Moving with Kids

25 Ways
to Ease Your
Family's Transition
to a
New Home

LORI COLLINS BURGAN

FOREWORD BY VIRGINIA L. MASON

The Harvard Common Press

BOSTON, MASSACHUSETTS

The Harvard Common Press
535 Albany Street
Boston, Massachusetts 02118
www.harvardcommonpress.com

Printed in the United States of America
Printed on acid-free paper

Library of Congress Cataloging-in-Publication Data
Burgan, Lori Collins.
    Moving with kids: 25 ways to ease your family's transition to a new home/Lori Collins Burgan.
        p. cm.
    Includes index.
    ISBN 1-55832-343-0 (pbk. : alk. paper)—ISBN 1-55832-342-2 (hardcover : alk. paper)
    1. Moving, Household—Psychological aspects. 2. Child psychology. 3. Parent and child.
    I. Title.
    TX307.B87 2007
    648'.90019—dc22   2006016734

ISBN-13: 978-1-55832-342-1 (hardcover); 978-1-55832-343-8 (paperback)
ISBN-10: 1-55832-342-2 (hardcover); 1-55832-343-0 (paperback)

Special bulk-order discounts are available on this and other Harvard Common Press books. Companies and organizations may purchase books for premiums or resale, or may arrange a custom edition, by contacting the Marketing Director at the address above.

Cover design by Night & Day Design
Interior design by Jill Winitzer
Cover illustration by Neverne Covington

10 9 8 7 6 5 4 3 2

To my phenomenal children, Rebecca, Sarah, and Mark, who make me thankful each day that I chose to be a parent. I admire each one of you more than you'll ever know.

To my husband, Randy, a private person who isn't totally comfortable with my sharing all our family stories in this book, but who supports my passion to do so.

To my dear friend Catherine Heaslip, who suggested that I write this book. I don't think I would have thought of it had you not planted the seed.

To Connie Williamson, Laurie Fike, Mary Olsen, Lisa Sullivan, K.C. Gullett, Debby Wadas, Roxann Ringnald, and Sherry Martinez for letting me share your stories.

Contents

Foreword

Moving is a fact of American life, and children are greatly affected. Parents, relatives, families with new foster and adopted children, and other caregivers need all of the information that Lori Collins Burgan has organized. They need her hope, and her realism about the grieving process that is inherent in every major life change. They need to understand the balance between loss and gain, between reality and expectation, and the need to help children maintain connections.

The irony of my promoting this book as a family-support professional is that I moved my family often—first as a military wife for ten years, and then, following my husband's death in a helicopter crash, as a widow whose career brought more moves. I wish I had been given this book when my children were young; I would have done a better job of empowering them. My grown daughter would say that she has weathered her adulthood with more hope and stability because the moves trained her to adapt. But she would also say that the moves were traumatic and painful. The moving was all that moving is: wonderful, exciting, frightening, and an opportunity to look at the world, for a time, through the filter of newness. Moving can be a way of animating the essential pioneer spirit in ourselves and in our families.

After I remarried and moved my children six times in a few years, our family landed in Evanston, Illinois, where we have been for ten years. During these seemingly stable years, I have moved four older children from orphanages in Russia to the United States and into my home, without thinking in a focused way about all of the excitement, hope, change, and grieving that the moves entailed for each child. The strength of older adopted children in facing a new culture and language on top of the loss of all that is familiar is a monument to the human spirit. Each child responds individually. One adopted daughter still grieves the loss of her best friend in a Russian orphanage. An adopted son is now "moving" to independence, and the book has illuminated the difficulty of that experience for a boy who had only a short time in a family after years of institutional living. The idea in this book of being an energy-generating parent with a sense of humor and positive expectations is absolutely key.

In recent years my older children have recounted moving stories from our past with real pleasure. They tell about a night in Tucumcari, New Mexico, during a move to Kansas, in which the wind was so strong and the weather so cold that our motel room could not be warmed. This forced the entire family into one bed, heaped with blankets and coats. Laughter, jokes, and a sense of adventure prevailed until morning arrived, with a cobalt-blue sky and a new-fallen snow covering everything within sight. Over pancakes and breakfast in a warm little restaurant, the children declared the night as having been "the most fun ever."

Most powerful in our family history of moving is the story of our first adoption, in Jamaica. Not long after my first husband's death, I decided to make new connections to life by taking two children and moving to the Caribbean. Three of us left, five of us returned, and the connections to Jamaica will never be severed.

Family Support America promotes family strength, and *Moving with Kids* is an important resource for families. My children have said that parents are the key to the moving experience; if the parents see the adventure and are grounded in the here and now, the children will reflect that energy in the long run. This book fosters awareness that loss is part of the moving process. It shows how information and understanding can make moving with kids a more intentional, thoughtful, creative, and joyful process. This is a book about building strength, treating each family member with respect, creating and celebrating family history, keeping in touch, and enlarging our sense of belonging to many places. The book reminds us that we should reach out to newcomers and others who move, that moving is a chance to learn and practice new skills and to develop new stories, and that electronic communications can provide new ways of promoting human connections and reducing isolation. This is a book about hope, about the movement of the human heart from one place to another, and about the paradox that we must reach out and hold on at the same time.

VIRGINIA L. MASON
President and CEO, Family Support America
Mother of Eric, Amy, Joy, Andy, David, Brittany,
Alexandra, Diana, Timur, and Albina

Preface

In writing this book, I do not claim to be an expert on how moving affects all children, nor have I conducted surveys to determine steps that everyone should take to reduce the negative impact of a move. Rather, I offer practical tips that have worked for my friends, acquaintances, and family members as we have moved around the country. Some of these tips I have garnered the hard way, through trial and error. Many I have discovered by listening to my children's ideas and dreams.

My personal experience with moving began between third and fourth grade, when my family moved from Pittsburgh, Pennsylvania, to Anderson, Indiana. The move entailed my transfer from a predominantly Caucasian, Jewish, upper-income school to a predominantly African-American, lower-income one, where I was one of two white children in my class. Seven years after this move, with the pain still fresh in my memory, I wrote this poem:

My Enemy

The car was filled with a painful silence,
Each too involved in his own desolation to speak.
A thin sheet of darkness was falling upon the earth,
While the last traces of the sun's purple-orange rays lingered on.
The car, as if with a mind of its own, was headed west,
To that flat, alien land, Indiana.
I had never seen Indiana,
But it was my enemy . . .
It was taking me away from my beloved home, Pittsburgh.
To those unknowing individuals,
Pittsburgh is a dirty, polluted steel-producing place,
But to me, it was all I had ever known.
It was my life.
I recalled:
The peacefulness of the three rivers as darkness crept into the air
And they illuminated it.
The pleasure and excitement as Roberto Clemente hit that
Game-winning home run over the fence at Three Rivers Park.
My very best friend, Cathy, who played Barbies with me for hours
And made me jealous when she got go-go boots before me.
Howard, my boyfriend, who made me cry in first grade
Because he kissed me—that was a no-no!
All these significant things being rudely snatched from my hands,
And I was only a child.
How could I realize the great happiness that awaited me?
Unaware, I stared out the window,
Watching the scene grow stranger, colder, darker,
And uninviting.

As young adults pursuing our careers, my husband, Randy, and I made several moves, from Anderson to Indianapolis, from Indianapolis to Chicago, and then to Louisville. We began putting down roots in Louisville, where our three children—Rebecca, Sarah, and Mark—were born. After Mark's birth, I wanted to take a break from my career to spend more time raising our children, so Randy and I decided to follow his career for a while. As soon as Randy's company learned he was willing to relocate, we were immediately transferred to Fort Lauderdale. After 16 months, Randy was asked to take a new position in Atlanta. After another 16 months, he was asked to move again, to the corporate head-quarters in Topeka. And after—you guessed it—another 16 months, we were asked to move to Baltimore. Intending Baltimore to be our permanent home, we built a house and spent three years developing what we thought would be long-term roots. But after a corporate restructuring resulting from the September 11th tragedy, the company gave Randy the option of moving back to Florida or taking a severance package. Once again, we made the heart-wrenching decision to move. We have been settled in the Tampa area since then. And although we plan to stay where we are for a long time, I have learned to never say never. (At one point in my life, I swore I'd never live in either Florida or Topeka!)

During one of our moves, I decided to see if I could find a help-ful source of ideas for making a move easier for children. I was surprised to find no such resources on the shelves of the three local bookstores that I visited. When I asked a clerk at a national bookstore chain to do a computer search for a book on moving with children, she found one, which I promptly ordered. It was long and written from a psychologist's perspective, using termi-nology that I was familiar with from my social-work training but that didn't seem to speak directly to concerned parents. The last thing I wanted to do while in the throes of a move was to delve into a complex book that would cause me even more stress. In the midst of my chaotic life, I was less interested in contemplating the psychological ramifications this move might have on my chil-dren's long-term development (although, granted, minimizing the long-term trauma is my ultimate goal) and more interested in finding answers to my prayer: "Dear God, help my kids and me make it through another day! And, by the way, could you do it in 200 words or less?"

Since I couldn't find the type of help I was looking for, I decided to follow one of the principles I have adopted in adjusting to moves:

If the resource you need isn't there, take a leadership role in creating it. Thus, the idea for this book was born.

The advice I offer here reflects not only my personal experiences and those of my children but also the experiences of other families who have moved a lot. I conducted in-depth interviews with five parents:

- Connie Williamson, a single mom who moved with her four sons three times in three years (the first move came within two weeks of the devastating news that resulted in the dissolution of her 19-year marriage).

- K.C. Gullett, a stay-at-home father of three who made two moves as primary caregiver while his family followed his wife's career.

- Laurie Fike, a homeschooling mother of two and the wife of an Air Force major, who has moved with her children five times, including once overseas to Germany.

- Mary Olsen, a mother of four and the wife of a Navy SEAL, whose family has moved seven times in 12 years—to Italy, Panama, and Guam as well as various parts of the United States.

- Lisa Sullivan, a mother of three and the wife of another Navy SEAL, whose family has moved six times in 10 years, including once overseas to Italy.

My children and I went into the past five moves grieving, lonely, and scared (Randy might say I went "kicking and screaming," but I'm sure that would be an exaggeration), and we came out of them not only calling each new home *home* but also liking it even more than our previous place of residence. I have come to believe, at the innermost core of my being, that home is truly where the heart is. And I can honestly say that my children, my husband, and I are a stronger, closer, better-rounded, and more content family because of all the moves we have made.

Introduction

Moving opens new doors—to new friendships, new opportunities, new forms of contentment. Through a move, your children can experience life-changing benefits that otherwise would not have been possible. Before they can begin to reap these bountiful rewards and unexpected blessings, however, you have to help your children deal with the unavoidable pain of leaving loved ones, familiar places, and memorable events behind.

Certain major milestones are expected in almost every move. These are the events that you prepare for: watching as the For Sale sign appears in the yard, attending goodbye parties, and walking through an empty house after all your belongings have been removed. For me, probably the most traumatic of these milestones has been helplessly standing by as my children have walked into classrooms filled with strangers. The fear and loneliness so transparent on my children's faces has been almost unbearable.

Although such expected milestones bring pain and sadness, being able to brace yourself and your children for them makes them more tolerable. It's the unexpected, seemingly inconsequential events that cause a stab of pain so intense it makes you stop in your tracks and grab your stomach to lessen the emptiness and hurt.

The screaming and chaos on the school bus suddenly stops, replaced by an eerie silence, as eight-year-old Rebecca gets off on her last day of school before moving to a new city 700 miles away. As she sullenly walks toward her house, her classmates spontaneously stick their heads out the windows and yell in unison, "Bye, Rebecca, we'll miss you."

On a Sunday evening two months after a move, seven-year-old Sarah gets a call from the best friend she had to leave behind. The friend's mother explains to me that her daughter just spent her birthday crying because she misses Sarah so much.

Three months after a move, five-year-old Mark—tired of playing with Mom all day—throws himself on the sofa and softly proclaims, "I miss my friends in Kansas. I wish we'd never moved."

One month later, Mark and I go to have pizza for lunch and the waitress mistakenly directs us to a table where several moms excitedly talk together while their children play. "No," I correct her as Mark looks at the other children longingly, "it's just the two of us eating together today."

Moving creates pain for the individual and the family, regardless of the circumstances. Whether a move is predominantly positive (to accept a job promotion, to be closer to family members) or negative (to find a new job after a layoff, to provide distance from a death or divorce), moving always produces stress and discomfort. The key is learning to embrace the pain: Feel it, accept it, and then move on from it. Many adults have learned coping skills that help them embrace the pain of moving without being enveloped by it. Our responsibility as parents is first to practice these healthy coping mechanisms ourselves, and then to teach them to our children.

Once you and your children have acknowledged the pain of moving and felt it, you can move on—to the awaiting friendships, new opportunities, and untapped happiness that come with a move to a new home. This book will show you how to make your relocation easier on your children, with the ultimate goal of turning the "enemy"—the move—into a family friend.

Make sure they hear it from you first.

At a recent social gathering, I stood in a group of eight adults listening to one acquaintance discuss an upcoming job relocation that he and his wife had decided to accept. After providing ample details, he added, almost as an afterthought, "Oh, and by the way, don't mention anything about this to my kids—we haven't told them yet." I never heard the ending to this story, but it is a safe bet that this man's children heard about their move through the grapevine before they heard it from their parents. It was poor judgment on the part of this man to think he could tell a secret to such a broad circle of acquaintances and not have it repeated to others. I've learned that it is important to have enough respect for your children and their feelings to make sure they learn about an upcoming move from you and your spouse in a private family setting. Children are extremely perceptive. They can generally tell when something out of the norm is taking place. The tension that fills your home while you are deliberating about a move is hard to hide. Children notice when your patience is diminished, when you get angry more easily, and when you are sullen. My seven-year-old daughter caught me off-guard before one move when she commented, "Mom, you don't seem as happy lately as you usually do." And I thought I was doing a good job covering up my heightened stress level!

Children also have amazing, albeit selective, listening skills. My daughter Rebecca may be deep in concentration while reading a book in the back of the house, but, as soon as I lower my voice in the kitchen to whisper a secret to a good friend, Rebecca saunters into the kitchen to get a drink of water. The more quietly I talk, the more intently my children seem to listen. Don't fool yourself into believing that your children don't notice the hushed conversations you are having with your spouse and close friends. They *do* notice, and they are listening carefully for clues regarding what is taking place. Children trust their parents to keep them apprised of important information that affects their lives. This trust is damaged if children figure out that their parents are planning a move before the parents take the time to tell them.

> "Every time we move, my mom and dad hold a family conference before they decide anything. At the conference we talk about who wants to move and things like that. It makes me happy that my parents let us talk about it."
>
> MARK, AGE 10

You will have to consider your particular circumstances when determining at what point in the process to let your children know about a potential move. Obviously, if you have older children and have decided to let them participate in making the decision to move or not, they will need to be informed as soon as the possibility of a move has surfaced. I know several families who have given each member an equal vote in the decision to move. To vote wisely, these children had to be kept fully informed from the beginning of the process.

Children of military families have no power to prevent a move, but they can often have some say over *where* the family moves. Laurie's children enjoy helping their parents fill out the Air

Force's "dream sheet," where the family lists the five places to which they would most like to move. Military employees and service members are often told well in advance where they might be moving, but the three military moms I interviewed never pass this information on to their children until they get official orders, because preliminary plans often change.

As a general rule, children who will not be involved in deciding whether to move probably shouldn't be told of a possible move until the plan becomes definite. To some parents, waiting to tell the children about a potential move may seem deceitful. I would argue, however, that it isn't fair to make children live with the stress of a move that may not even happen.

If there is a chance that your children will learn about a potential move from some other source, however, you should err on the side of caution by telling them right away. Stress that the move is only a possibility and that nothing in their lives needs to change for the moment. You can probably avoid this situation if, until you have told your children, you discuss the potential move only with close friends and family members whom you know you can trust. A casual acquaintance is sure to know a neighbor who has a sister who . . . well, you get the picture.

If changes are coming quickly, you may find it best to keep your children informed every step of the way. Connie was enjoying being a stay-at-home mom in Indiana when, after 19 years of marriage, her husband blind-sided her with news that led to the abrupt end of their union. She and her husband immediately told their four boys that they would be getting a divorce. Because the marriage was ending so unexpectedly, Connie felt it was critical not to let her sons have any more surprises. Anxious to get a job that could support her and her children, Connie explained to the boys that she would be interviewing for a job that might necessitate a move out of state. She gave them updates—including bad news and tentative information—as soon as she could. The warnings were none too early, because exactly two weeks after her husband's revelation Connie accepted a position in Nashville and moved there with her sons.

Because an announcement of a move is usually traumatic, it is important to choose carefully not only the timing but also the setting. Children need to be able to digest the information in an environment in which they feel safe expressing whatever emotions may surface—anger, denial, sadness, fear, excitement, or indifference. Randy and I have generally called a family meeting to discuss an impending move; we set aside the entire evening to discuss the matter with the children. Before you make your announcement, make sure you can give your children your undivided attention: Clear your appointment calendar, turn off the television, ignore the doorbell, and let the answering machine get the phone. Your children need to know that you realize that this decision will greatly affect the rest of their lives. Your willingness to help them come to terms with the change must be a priority.

A final word of advice: If you move often, don't call family meetings only to announce a move—the kids will catch on! Several years ago, before we could begin one of our meetings to inform the kids of an upcoming move, our middle child blurted out, "I bet we're going to move again!" Since then, Randy and I have devised other reasons for periodic family meetings.

2

Empower your children to make as many decisions as possible.

The strongest principle of growth lies in human choice.

—George Eliot, *Daniel Deronda*

Children generally can't choose whether or not to move. Their parents may view a move as positive or negative, but in either case it is forced upon the children. The feeling of powerlessness that results can be overwhelming for a child. Throughout the process of moving, therefore, it is important to find ways to let children exercise some control.

Maybe they can have some say over the timing of a move. They might rather wait and finish the year at their old school instead of starting mid-semester at a new one. Or maybe they'd rather get the move over with as soon as possible and begin making new friends.

How about giving your children some say in selecting the type of neighborhood you will live in? Would they be more comfortable in a subdivision with a lot of children? Or would they enjoy getting a house in the country with land to explore? Would they like an apartment within walking distance of school? Or a townhouse from which they would get to ride a bus to school?

Even children as young as three can make some decisions about a move. They can pick which toys they want to take with them for the trip or for a stay in temporary housing and which ones they don't mind packing into boxes for the new home. Would they like to take their old swing set, or buy a new one for the new yard? How would they like to decorate their new room? What color would they like their new room to be painted? Would they like to be the one to tell their friends they are moving, or would they rather have Mom or Dad do it?

When Randy and I hold a family meeting to tell our children about an upcoming move, we spend as much time as necessary letting everyone express their feelings about the changes that will occur. When the children are ready, we then move on to the task-oriented part of the agenda. We have paper and pencils ready, and one child is chosen as the recorder. (During a stage when the kids enjoyed playing school, we used a flip chart to record our notes.)

> "Being able to make important decisions related to our move has definitely helped me to cope with the transitions and has given me control in times when I feel most helpless."
>
> REBECCA, AGE 14

First we make a list of all the questions the children have about the move itself and the new area to which we'll be moving. Even if Randy and I know the answers, we write down each question instead of answering right away. When our children were young, their questions were relatively simple: "Do they have trees in Kansas?" (Uh . . . not many!) "What are the schools like?" "Are the teachers nice?" "Is there a Godfather's Pizza?" "What other restaurants are there?" "What kinds of things are there for children to do?" "Are we going to drive or fly there?" "Can we take our hamster?" Once they got older, their questions became harder to answer: "Will I get to come back and visit my old friends?" "How will I find a good flute teacher?" "What is the tryout schedule for soccer teams?" "What if my classes at the new school are more or less advanced than my classes here?"

When the children have run out of questions, we talk about the ones to which Randy and I already know the answers, and we commit to finding answers to the remaining ones. Randy and I generally plan a trip to the new area without the children, to explore the surroundings, determine which city and neighborhood we want to settle in, and look for a house. An important item on the to-do list for this trip is getting answers to all of the questions posed at the family meeting.

The second agenda item at our family meeting is making a list of all the features the children would like in a new house and neighborhood. We discuss the things we have liked the most and least about our previous residences. Randy and I listen carefully and write down all the children's suggestions. We stress to the children that we likely will not be able to meet all their expectations, and that they will have to trust us to make the best choices possible, taking into consideration all the variables involved.

For example, we lived on a friendly cul-de-sac in Louisville, Kentucky, with so many children and pets that driving down the street was like going through an obstacle course. On all subsequent moves, our children asked us to find another house on a cul-de-sac. In each of our first three moves, unfortunately, such a house was unavailable in the time frame, price range, or neighborhood we wanted. We had to explain this to the children, after making sure that many of their other wishes were fulfilled. In our moves to Baltimore and Tampa, we were able to find cul-de-sac homes. During our most recent move, Randy and I narrowed the house choices down to three, and we actually let the children decide which of those three houses we would buy.

Once the major decision to move has been made, there are hundreds of little decisions along the way in which children can have some say. Some children—and some parents—care more about schools and extracurricular activities than about the immediate neighborhood of the prospective home. Mary, a military mom, often gives her children a choice about which school they will attend. During one move, she thoroughly researched the schools in the region and selected a home in an area known for its strong public schools, even though this meant an hour-and-a-half drive to work for her husband. When her daughter was visibly uncomfortable during a visit to the public middle school, Mary did more research. Undeterred by the inconvenience of having to drive her children to school each day, Mary chose a small parochial school at which her daughter felt more at ease.

Mary feels it is critical to allow her children some say not only about where they go to school but also about what they do after school. Shortly after a move, Mary asks her older children to prepare a prioritized list of the extracurricular activities in which they want to be involved. Then she makes sure that at least their top desires are met.

Although Connie had only two weeks from conception to execution of her first move as a single mom, she let her four sons partic-

DECISIONS CHILDREN CAN HELP MAKE

Are we going to move?

What time of year will be best for the move?

What kind of going-away party should we have?

In what type of neighborhood (urban, suburban, rural) would we like to live?

What features are important to us in a new house?

What toys or other items would we like to keep with us on the moving trip?

How shall we decorate the new bedroom?

What academic standards and offerings would we like in a new school?

What enrichment activities (such as orchestra, soccer, or drama) would we like the new school to offer?

What activities (such as scouting, community theater, or a sport) would we like to be involved in outside of school?

ipate in several related decisions. The children convinced her to select a home close to the few families they knew in Nashville rather than closer to her workplace, which was thirty miles away. Because the boys didn't want to live in an apartment, Connie rented a house. After they had been in Nashville for a year, Connie's sons urged her to rent a different house, one that would allow them each a little more privacy. Although Connie didn't feel up to yet another move, she agreed out of respect for her sons' needs and wishes. In return, the boys agreed to do their fair share of the physical work of moving.

As much as you value your children's opinions, you'll want to avoid pretending that everyone in the family has an equal vote in all the decisions about moving. As a parent, you have the wisdom and foresight to understand the ramifications of each option much better than your children do. Still, there are many decisions your children can safely make during and following a move. Don't assume you know what choices they will make--they'll often surprise you. And even when you really do know their preferences, give them the opportunity to express their opinions anyway. Tell them how important their views are to you, and make sure they know that their preferences have taken priority in some decisions. This will help them feel they have regained some control over a situation in which they at first felt powerless.

3

Let family priorities guide your decision making.

In your lifetime, there may be only two or three watershed moments in which you have the opportunity to prove the strength of your character.

If someone asked you and your partner right now what your family's number-one priority is, how long would it take you to come up with an answer? More important, would you both give the same answer?

Just as a successful business consists of employees working together for the same purpose, a well-functioning family should be guided by an agreed-upon set of values and priorities. Hopefully, you and your partner have talked at length about what's important to you in your family life. If you are a single parent, you have probably spent time on your own thinking through your priorities for your family. These priorities should be the directing force when you face critical decisions that will affect your family, including whether or not to make a move.

Let me pause at this point to add a note of clarification: In some instances, moving is the only acceptable option. For example, if the choice is between moving for a job or ending up on the welfare rolls, then moving is the responsible thing to do. Likewise, military families have signed on to go wherever and whenever the government tells them. Their first priority, then, is keeping their commitment to serve their country. As Mary, the wife of a Navy SEAL, explains, "We have a speech that we give each time we tell the kids we are moving: 'Kids, we're a Navy family. The country needs your father to help protect us, and we have to do our part for the country by going wherever the Navy sends us.'" (As the result of many moves, Mary's family has learned the value of experiencing different cultures, meeting wonderful people across the world, and appreciating the beauty each place has to offer. This value may become a priority in the future, when the family has a real choice about moving.)

When you have the option to move or not, your decision will depend on any number of family priorities. Maybe you live close to your parents and want to sustain your children's close relationship with their grandparents. Or maybe your elderly parent needs daily care, and you are unwilling to turn this responsibility over to a paid stranger. Maybe you couldn't afford to go to college yourself, and so you're determined that you will make enough money to ensure your children get a college education. Or maybe your children are in high school, and you have committed to making sure their schooling is uninterrupted until they graduate.

K.C. and his wife, Lynette, were frustrated with their hectic lives in Chicago, where they had full-time jobs that kept them out until 7:30 each night and allowed them little peaceful time with their children. When Lynette was offered a new job with higher pay, they had lengthy discussions about their family priorities. They decided that Lynette would accept the new position, although this would mean moving. With the extra money Lynette would make, they would be able to afford to have K.C. stay home with the kids. The prospective improvement in the family's quality of life was a much higher priority for Lynette and K.C. than the inconvenience of a move, even though they would be farther away from their extended family. Not only would the children get to stay home with their father instead of being cared for by a babysitter, but they would also benefit from having a more rested and focused mother who wouldn't have to spend her weekends doing household chores and errands, because K.C. would be able to take care of those things during the week.

A family's priorities will change as family dynamics change. When Randy and I first got married, for example, one of our priorities was to establish fulfilling, worthwhile careers. Eight years into our marriage, when we began having children, a bigger priority was balancing our well-established careers with our desire to be as involved as possible in our children's lives. To fulfill this commitment, we used the money we might have spent on a larger house to hire a nanny to care for the children in our home. Our priorities changed again after our third child was born, when I wanted to take a break from my career and spend more time with the children. To make up for the loss in income, Randy and I decided that he should aggressively pursue promotion opportunities through his company. Little did we realize that this would involve making five moves in the course of seven years. Yet, as we embarked on each move, we reminded ourselves that we were being true to our family's priorities.

Once we moved to Baltimore, Randy and I decided that our priority would be to secure our financial situation so that we would be free to choose not to move in the future without jeopardizing our financial stability. This priority was put to the test in November 2001, when Randy's company told us we'd have to move to Florida if he wanted to keep his job. Because we had just begun our financial plan, we couldn't turn down the move without serious consequences. So we called a family meeting and presented the kids with our options: (1) We could move to Florida and maintain our standard of living; (2) we could stay in Baltimore, Randy could find a lesser-paying job, I would go back to work full time, and we would tighten our belts as necessary; or (3) the kids and I could stay in Baltimore while Randy moved to Florida and flew home on weekends. Based on our positive experiences with previous moves, we all agreed—after much discussion—that the first option was the best for our family.

Two years after our move to Tampa, our family priorities were tested again when Randy was offered his dream job, which would require another move. This time we were further along with our financial plan, the kids were getting older and more settled (particularly Rebecca, who was very happy in the local high school), and Randy knew he could keep his existing job if he turned down the dream one. So once again we called a family meeting and painstakingly discussed the options. And while we agreed that the move would be best from a financial perspective, we also felt certain that the best thing for the overall health and happiness of our family at this point would be to stay where we were. This was a watershed moment for our family. Randy's willingness to surrender his own dreams for the best interests of our family was the ultimate test, in my opinion, of the strength of his character.

> **"Moving definitely gets harder as you get older, because you get more attached to your friends, your school, and your lifestyle."**
>
> MIKE, AGE 15

Likewise, Connie had to change her family priorities as her family dynamics changed. When she first found out that she would be getting a divorce and thus would become the primary provider for her four boys, Connie chose to move to Nashville for a well-paying job. Once she proved herself in the Nashville job and developed more salability as an employee, her priority became to provide her sons regular contact with their father. So she looked for and finally took a comparable job in Indiana, where her ex-husband lived. With the move to Indiana, Connie was able to meet her sons' needs both for financial security and for a more stable relationship with their father.

As long as your set of priorities works for your family, don't worry about what anyone else thinks of it. A good friend of mine decided several years ago that her continual traveling was taking too high a toll on her husband and children, so she sought out a lower-paying job that required minimal travel. To this day, she has colleagues who are convinced she was demoted involuntarily. My friend knows she made the right decision for her family, regardless of the rumors to which she was subjected.

Sometimes your family priorities may be tested in ways that surprise you. My friends Paul and Roxann Ringnald made 13 moves with Paul's job while they were raising their two sons, without ever feeling that they were sacrificing their chief priority of a secure, stable life for their children. When their sons were 18 and 21, Paul was offered the promotion for which he had been working his whole career. The promotion would require a move, but, since their sons were grown, the time seemed ideal for it. For the first time, though, a move just didn't feel right to Paul and Roxann. Their older son, Joe, was trying to establish his career, and Lance, their younger son, had competed on the U.S. gymnastics team in the 1988 Olympics and was in training for the 1992 competition. As Roxann explained, "To move at this point felt like we'd be taking the safety net away from Joe and the emotional support away from Lance at a time when they needed it the most. We felt we needed to stay where we were a touchstone for our kids . . . to bring some stability to their lives." Even with their children grown and trying to test their independence, Paul and Roxann knew that staying true to their family priorities meant that they must turn down this long-awaited promotion.

Fortunately for the Ringnalds, Paul's company offered him the promotion again several years later, and this time he accepted, sure that his sons were now ready to make it on their own (Lance made the U.S. Olympic gymnastics team again in 1992 and was recently inducted into the USA Gymnastics Hall of Fame). But many people who have turned down job promotions have never been offered another, or, even worse, have ended up being "phased out" of their existing jobs because their refusal to move meant they were no longer seen as "team players." When you refuse to compromise your family priorities, you have to be absolutely sure you're willing to live with the consequences. Of course, if your decision about a move conflicts with your family's core values, you have to be prepared to live with the consequences of that as well.

4

Do your research.

*Before anything else,
preparation is the key to success.*
—Alexander Graham Bell

Choosing the neighborhood that is the best fit for your family is one of the most critical decisions you will make when moving. If you have a choice about whether or not to move, research the economic situation of the area to which you might go. For example, a 15 percent salary increase may sound enticing, but if the cost of living in the new community is 20 percent higher than where you are living now, then—from a financial viewpoint—moving is not a good idea. Web sites such as www.homefair.com and www.realtor.com provide comparative information on communities across the country, using indicators that include cost of living and median household income. In researching costs, make sure you consider not just housing costs but also expenses such as state income taxes, property taxes, sales taxes, utility costs, and insurance rates.

When your decision to move is final, it's time to determine the parameters of your housing search. How far away from work are you willing to live? What is your housing price range? What are your children's educational or child-care needs? Although you certainly want to find the best possible house for the money, a higher priority is likely finding the neighborhood that best fits your family's needs.

For my family, determining the right community always begins with research into the public schools. When we decided to move to Florida the second time, we knew we could live anywhere in the state, because Randy's job would have him traveling all over it. Randy had to begin his job in Florida eight months before we could move the household, so we had plenty of time to pinpoint the areas that we felt were the most family-friendly. Once a week after work, Randy would visit a real-estate agent to identify prospective neighborhoods in whichever part of the state he was working that week. He would call me afterward with the names of schools

---

MATTERS TO RESEARCH BEFORE A MOVE

The cost of living in the new community relative to the cost of living where you are

The quality of academic instruction at prospective schools

The availability and quality of enrichment activities (sports, music, clubs, etc.) at prospective schools

The availability of transportation to school, and the length of the bus ride

The availability and quality of daycare or after-school care

The suitability of prospective neighborhoods, including prospects for playmates and family activities

The proximity of a suitable church, temple, or mosque

Local amenities (public library, parks, swimming pool, scouting, and other youth organizations)

in those neighborhoods, and I would promptly research the schools on the Internet. The Florida Department of Education, like many states, has a Web site with "report cards" for every school in the state (the Web site www.realtor.com also provides general information about schools in most areas of the country). The Florida site includes not only students' average test scores and other academic indicators for each school but also social indicators, such as incidences of drug use and violence, dropout rates, and graduation rates. Within five minutes, I could determine whether the school was a place where I would be comfortable sending my children.

I likely ruled out many good schools through the use of school report cards, which do not always accurately reflect the quality of education. These report cards are a time- and cost-effective tool when you're choosing a community, but it is important to consider which indicators make up the school grade and to ask the Department of Education for more information as appropriate. If a school seems like a good one, find out some details that matter to your children, by either calling the school or examining the school's Web site. Maybe only one of the many schools in your targeted area has an orchestra. Maybe football is popular at all schools in a district, but only a few have soccer programs. If your child has been studying a foreign language, you might want to find out whether it's offered at the school you're considering. Ditto for advanced or special-education programs. Look into the quality of the drama programs or debate teams, if these are activities that interest your children. Find out whether the school has a Parent Teacher Association, or ask how much parent involvement is welcome. If you like most aspects of a school but it is lacking in a key area, check whether a public or private non-school organization can make up for the deficiency.

Through a process of elimination, Randy and I were eventually

> "In the military when they tell you where you are going to move, they give you the name of a sponsor who already lives there. I spend a lot of time sending e-mails to the sponsor before we move. We do a lot of Internet research, too, but it's helpful to get information from someone who's actually living there."
>
> LAURIE, MOTHER OF TWO

able to find a Florida community that met our priorities: (1) neighborhood schools with parental involvement at all grade levels, (2) strong academic records and low rates of drug use and violence, (3) fast growth, so our children wouldn't be the only new kids, and (4) proximity to my grandparents' home (this was important because we would be more than a thousand miles from both my parents and Randy's).

Now, before you dismiss the concept of research because you don't have the luxury of spending eight months looking for a new home, let me point out that most of our housing decisions have been made over a long weekend. For example, Randy and I had four days to determine where we wanted to live in the metropolitan Baltimore area and to actually buy a house. At the end of the third day we were ready to make an offer on what seemed the perfect house, but first we visited the local school and were devastated to realize it wouldn't be a good fit for our kids. So we had to start from scratch on the fourth and final day. We did end up finding a good house and school, but we came close to reconsidering the whole move because we weren't willing to settle for something that wouldn't meet our children's needs.

Condensed searches can be successful if you—

• Conduct extensive Internet research in advance. Most cities and counties have Web sites, and real-estate companies advertise on the Internet and can e-mail detailed information about particular houses. Before choosing an agent to work with, interview several. Before you visit, talk at length with the agent you have chosen to make sure your family's needs and priorities are understood.

• Go prepared to expend a lot of energy. Randy and I warn our real-estate agents in advance that we want to see 20 houses a day and have no interest in socializing over long, leisurely lunches until our task is accomplished!

• Be assertive in asking questions and probing areas of interest and importance to your family when dealing with both real-estate agents and school personnel.

If education or child care is your first priority, then start your research there. Even if your children are too young for school or you are homeschooling them, it is important to research the school system in case you decide to use it in the future. Schedule your house-hunting trip for a time when you can visit schools (during the summer, the principal may be available to meet with you, especially if you make an appointment before your trip). If you aren't able to visit the area before you move, then call and talk to the principal or guidance counselor. Have your list of questions ready, including your children's. Don't forget to visit or call the school or schools your children would attend when they get older. And don't hesitate to dig for information. During a school visit in a small community, I was able to convince the school secretary to tell me the number of kids—by grade and address—in the neighborhood we were considering so that I could determine whether there would be enough prospective friends for my children!

When you inquire about schools, get the details confirmed. For example, a school close to your house might not be your child's assigned school. Sometimes larger communities bus children out of their immediate neighborhoods, and smaller communities faced with population declines sometimes have to close their local schools and bus the children to neighboring communities. Be specific in your questions about the mode of transportation to school and the length of rides. When we moved to Fort Lauderdale, a school secretary told me that bus transportation would be provided for any child living more than one mile from the school. Becca was excited about riding the bus to kindergarten from our house, which was a mile and a half away from the school. But a few days before school started, when I called to find out where and when the bus stopped, the same secretary told me that the mile was measured "as the crow flies" and not as driving distance. Needless to say, Becca was very disappointed, and I was faced with two extra car trips each day.

Once you determine which schools you are willing to consider, your research into housing options can focus on other issues that are important to you. For instance—

Which neighborhoods have children similar in age to yours? (We have
actually sat at bus stops after school dismissal time and counted
kids getting off in prospective neighborhoods. Lisa, a military mom,
walks through neighborhoods and counts basketball hoops, trampolines, and play sets.)

What are the traffic patterns? Will walking and bike-riding on the roads
be safe enough for your children?

What places of worship are available? Attend a service, if you have
time.

What amenities (such as tennis courts, playgrounds, pools, and walking
and biking trails) do various neighborhoods offer?

As you're conducting your research, don't forget to check into
all the services and facilities that are important to your family.
Determining whether there are good after-school or daycare programs could be critical. Find out whether there is a public library,
and whom it serves (in some areas, people who live outside the city
limits can't borrow books without paying a fee). Is there a public
swimming pool, a YMCA, a Boys and Girls Club? Are there scouting programs? Are there parks close by? If so, are they clean and
appealing to children, with intact play equipment and shaded
areas?

When military families are told to move, they often know people already living in the assigned community. In addition, the military generally assigns a sponsor to answer questions and help the
family get settled. If you're making a military move, take advantage of these resources. Particularly if you're moving overseas,
ask your sponsor or friends at the destination base what the
schools are like, what places of worship are available, which hospi-
tals have personnel who speak English, and what you can expect
in a rented or purchased house or apartment. An "unfurnished"
house overseas, for example, may lack not only furniture but also
kitchen cabinets, light fixtures, medicine cabinets, and window
screens! Before Laurie's family moved to Tampa, their sponsor
gave Laurie information on local homeschool groups. Laurie

e-mailed one of the groups to connect her children with a home-schooling pen pal whom they could look forward to meeting after the move.

If you don't have the advantage of knowing someone living in the new community, initiate conversations with local people during your house-hunting trip. Visit a park, and ask a friendly parent what she or he likes about the community. Talk to a mom at the library about which dance schools or athletic programs she thinks are the best. Strike up a conversation with residents in a prospective neighborhood about local activities and events, such as festivals and parades. If you've decided you want to live in a rural community, this could mean walking down long driveways and knocking on doors (just watch out for aggressive dogs and No Trespassing signs). And don't forget to stop at the Chamber of Commerce, tourist information office, or city hall. These places are rich sources of information on services and resources available in the community.

Where you live determines how you live. Once you've purchased or rented a house or an apartment, you will have to live with your choice for a long time. Take advantage of the Internet and any local contacts you can find to learn as much as possible about the area before you move. Choosing the right community, neighborhood, and school district can help your children adapt much more quickly and smoothly to their new home.

5

Carefully consider when the move should take place.

> For everything there is a season,
> and a time for every purpose under heaven:
> a time to be born, and a time to die;
> a time to plant, and a time to
> pluck up that which is planted.
> —Ecclesiastes 3:1–2

Any real-estate agent can tell you that more people move during the summer than at any other time of the year. Conventional wisdom dictates that this is the best time for most families to move, because schedules are looser, school is out, and the pace of life is generally more relaxed. A move during the summer gives families a chance to settle in before the hectic pace of the school year begins.

In our first move with the children, we assumed that a summer move was the best alternative; we didn't really consider any other timing. When we completed our move in mid-June, however, we found that many of the neighborhood children were busy with camps and vacations. We also learned quickly that, because of the intense heat, summers in Florida are comparable to winters in northern climates—most people stay in their (air-conditioned) houses and venture out only when necessary. Therefore, it wasn't until the school year started that our children began to make friends and feel that Fort Lauderdale was their home. In the meantime, they spent a long two and a half months with no friends.

Determined to learn from our mistake, we made our move from Fort Lauderdale to Atlanta in mid-October, after the school year was under way. The transition was smoother and quicker. It was easier for the teachers to identify my children as new and to give them extra attention to help with their transition. The other children also took more notice of them and were quicker to offer friendship. When I picked Sarah up on the first day at her new preschool in Atlanta, her big brown eyes twinkled as she excitedly reported, "Mom, I got a lot of attention today!"

Realizing that we were on to something with the rationale for moving during the school year, we frantically rushed our move from Atlanta to Topeka so that we could get there with eight weeks of school remaining. The academic transition was a little difficult: My second-grader's new class was in the middle of a study on dinosaurs, which she knew nothing about; the style of printing was different; and the standard for speed in arithmetic was much higher than in her former school. In general, though, the children's transition was the quickest of any move. Within one week, Rebecca and Sarah were going on play dates and being invited to birthday parties. (Because it was so late in the school year, none of the preschools would let us enroll Mark, so his transition was rougher; he didn't start making friends until school started again in the fall.) Becca and Sarah immediately became so involved in sports, Brownies, and church activities that by the time summer came they were easily able to maintain their friendships, making them feel that they were already part of the crowd when the next school year began.

Because of these positive experiences with moving during the school year, I had originally titled this chapter "Move in the Middle of the School Year." Before I finished writing the book, however, we moved again, and I realized that just when I thought I had this all figured out I needed a little more education. At our November meeting to plan our move to Tampa, Randy and I asked the kids, "What can we do to make this move easier for you?" Becca, Sarah, and Mark unanimously agreed that the number-one thing we could do was to wait until the school year was over. After talking through this request, we realized that the attention they enjoyed as "new kids" when they were younger was now seen as a detriment. As preteens, they preferred to blend in with the crowd. So we honored their request and made our move to Tampa in June, even though this meant that Randy had to commute long-distance for eight months. To help ensure that the children wouldn't spend the summer without playmates, we moved to a subdivision that was under development so that there would be other "new kids" with whom our children could make friends.

> "Twice, I moved with the children several months before my husband could join us, so that they could have some time in school before summer began. Living apart from their dad was stressful for the kids, but we felt it was important to get them into the new school right away so they could begin making friends."
>
> LISA, MOTHER OF THREE

Like my family on our first move, K.C.'s family followed conventional wisdom and made their first move during the summer. They immediately questioned this choice, because the children found it difficult to make friends or get involved in organized activities until school started. So when K.C.'s wife was asked to move again, they decided to do it during the spring. With only one and a half months of school left when they moved to New Jersey, many of their friends questioned their judgment in changing schools so late in the school year. However, K.C. found that his children (who were still in elementary school) adjusted fine academically, and they had the benefit of being able to make a few friends before the summer began.

As is apparent in these examples, there is no rule of thumb to follow regarding the timing of a move. The best time will vary depending on your children's ages, personalities, and stages of development. In determining when a move should take place, listen to your children. Don't assume that summer is the best time because that's when most people move. And don't assume that a time of year that worked well once will work well for all subsequent moves. Your children's needs and desires will change as they grow older, and responding to those needs in a sensitive manner will help make the transition go more smoothly.

Of course, you may not have the luxury of deciding when the move will take place. You may be a single parent who has to move when the job is available, and your children may have to go when you go. Or you may be moving overseas, and the logistics necessitate that the whole family move together. In many situations, however, families have more leeway than they realize. For example, the closing date of your house sale may be nonnegotiable, but perhaps it would be possible for your family to move into temporary quarters. If your spouse needs to start a new job soon, perhaps you could stay with the children in your current community a little while longer. If your child is a teenager, he or she might even be comfortable staying with friends or relatives for a few weeks.

The timing of a move can be a critical tool in easing a child's transition to a new home. So put aside conventional wisdom and consider carefully when the move should take place to best meet the needs of your children.

6

Involve your children in plans for family pets.

Animals are such agreeable friends—
they ask no questions, they pass no criticisms.

—George Eliot, *Mr. Gilfil's Love Story*

As if you need one more thing to do in the midst of preparing for a move, planning for a pet's transition can take several weeks, or even months if your move will be overseas. But older children can help, both before and during a move. And once you're in your new home, your children will find it comforting to have their animal friend with them. Taking care of a pet can serve as a welcome distraction until your children have the chance to make new human friends.

The promise of a new pet can increase the appeal of a prospective move. We eased the transition from Topeka to Baltimore for Sarah by promising her we would fulfill her dream of owning a dog once we moved. The enticement of a canine companion gave her something to look forward to. Many families who know they may be sent overseas choose not to get a family pet so they can avoid having to leave it when they move (in fact, some dog breeders have refused to sell to military families because the breeders don't want their dogs to have to deal with the trauma of an overseas move). Other families consider temporary pet ownership. Laurie told her children when they moved to Germany that they could get a small pet as long as they understood they would have to find a home for it before they moved back to the United States. The children excitedly selected a guinea pig and a bunny, and taking care of the animals became something constructive for the children to do while they adjusted to living overseas. When their father's three-year stint was up, they were able to find loving homes for their pets through their homeschool contacts. Knowing they would not be moving overseas again, Laurie promised her children they could get a cat when they returned to the United States. As Laurie explains, "Knowing that she was going to get a cat when we moved to Florida kept Megan going. In fact, when our plane was landing we realized that she actually thought the cat would be waiting for her as soon as the plane hit the ground!"

If you already have a family pet, and it will be coming with you to your new home, you can use the following checklist to plan for your pet's move, assigning tasks to your children according to their maturity:

Determine how your pet will be transported. Because trains and buses don't allow pets other than service animals, your two choices will be air and car travel.

If air transportation is your first choice, find out the airline's rules about transporting animals. Computer-savvy children can be assigned the task of researching airline regulations. They will vary depending on the size of the animal, whether it will be accompanied or unaccompanied, and the time of the year. Be aware that in hotter months pets are not allowed to travel as air freight. During this time, if your pet is too large to fit in a carrier under your airplane seat, air travel will not be an option. Flight reservations for your pet should be made as far in advance as possible. Be sure to inquire about pet insurance, if you want it.

Learn about state, local, and, when you're moving abroad, national regulations regarding the entry and control of pets. Again, children who know how to use the computer can look online for regulations posted by the Office of the State Veterinarian and local animal-control agencies. Many states require that dogs and horses be accompanied by an interstate health certificate, and almost all states require that proof of a rabies vaccine be attached to a dog's collar.

Several weeks before the move, take your dog or cat to the veterinarian to make sure the animal's immunizations are current and to secure a health certificate and any other records you may need. You might also inquire about the possibility of sedating your pet for the trip.

A week before the move, make sure you have all the supplies you will need for transporting your pet, including an approved carrier, if necessary; a travel identification tag with emergency contact information for someone not traveling with you; and plenty of your pet's favorite foods (it's possible that your pet's favorite brand may not be available in your new location, and you'll want to provide familiar food through the adjustment period). If overnight travel by car will be required, make sure your lodging place allows pets.

The day before the move, involve your children in packing a travel bag for their pet. This bag might include food, treats, water, food and water bowls, a litter box (for a cat), a leash, favorite toys, a blanket, health certificates and medical records, a brush, medications, moistened wipes or paper towels for emergency cleanups, and airtight plastic bags for waste disposal.

The day of the move, a dog or cat may be aware that a change is taking place and may feel apprehensive. If your children are old enough, assign one of them to be in charge of the pet—taking care of him, comforting him, and keeping him safe. When you arrive at your new home, make sure all doors are closed before the pet is let out of the carrier.

Although a cat will probably want to hide under the furniture for a while, you can ask your children to give your dog a tour of the house, making sure some of his familiar toys are scattered around. Taking a dog for a walk on a leash through your new neighborhood is a great way to attract new friends.

Shortly after the move, find a new veterinarian for your animal. Even
though it may be a while before your pet needs a checkup, it is
important to identify a vet you can call to find out what the proce-
dures are for handling after-hours emergencies.

Moving with a pet overseas requires even more planning. Some
countries require a quarantine period of as long as six months for
an animal coming from another country (although there is sometimes flexibility in the quarantine period and conditions; you can
find out by talking with people in the quarantine office of your destination city). Not only is such a quarantine hard on the children
who care for a pet, but it also can be very expensive, sometimes
costing thousands of dollars. One well-organized mom, knowing
that the companionship of their dog would ease her children's
adjustment to a new home overseas, sent the dog several months
ahead of the family. Friends already living in the destination city
arranged for the dog's quarantine, so that the quarantine period
was over by the time the family arrived.

Small pets such as hamsters and gerbils usually travel rather easily in the cages that they live in at home. If you remove the water
container to avoid spills during travel, make sure you give the pet
fresh water each time you stop.

Birds may have more difficulty making a move. Put a cover over
the cage while they are traveling.

Moving fish can be risky, because changes in water temperature
and a lack of oxygen can kill them. If you must move fish, transfer
them to an unbreakable container filled with water from your
aquarium. In cold weather, you may need to put the container
into an insulated box. Make sure your children understand that
the fish may not survive the move. A better idea might be to
encourage your children to give the fish away before you move,
and then get new ones once you are settled in your new home.
You could sweeten this suggestion by offering to buy them a new
species that they covet, new aquarium decorations, or even a new,
larger aquarium after the move. When my son's best friend, Seth,

moved out of state, he didn't want to risk losing his pet fish during the trip. So Seth gave the fish to Mark and another friend, Brady, as a parting gift. Mark and Brady agreed to share the fish, each taking care of it for a certain period of time. This ended up being a great way for Mark and Brady to remember their friend Seth.

There may be circumstances in which you must leave behind a dog, a cat, or another pet to which your children are very attached. Your pet may have health problems that would make the move dangerous for him; you may be moving to a country where diseases or parasites could put him at risk; or you may be moving to a house or an apartment where pets are not permitted. Having to leave a pet can be a major blow for a child. Younger children might worry that they too may someday become a "dispensable" member of the family. Older children may feel angry at having to give up yet another beloved friend because of the move.

The decision to leave a pet behind will necessitate serious family discussion. It is important to be specific in explaining why the pet can't move with you. Ask your children for ideas about the type of new home that might make their pet happy, and for suggestions of friends who might want the animal. When a new home is found, bring the children with you to visit it, if possible, and point out its advantages for your pet. (For example, is there a large yard in which the dog can run free? Are there children who will treat the pet lovingly? Is there someone at home during the day to give the animal a lot of attention?)

> "When we moved to Maryland, I was feeling a bit sad about leaving Kansas, and I wanted a dog really bad. My parents decided that I could get a dog, so we got Gabi. Gabi is now five years old, and I'll never again be sad when I think about moving to Maryland, because that's how I got her."
>
> SARAH, AGE 13

Make sure your children have ample opportunity to say goodbye to a pet who must stay behind. They might exchange keepsakes with the animal; for example, they could leave one of their T-shirts as bedding for the pet, and take one of his toys as a remembrance. And don't forget to take lots of pictures. In chapter 12 are more tips on helping your children mourn the loss of loved ones, including pets, left behind as a result of moving.

Finally, one of the disadvantages of moving may be having to leave a pet's grave behind. Lisa, a military mom, came up with a meaningful solution to this problem. The night before she had to take her family's cancer-ridden dog to be put to sleep, Lisa made a steppingstone with the dog's paw prints around the edges and his favorite tennis ball in the middle. In remembrance of their dog, the family takes the steppingstone with them each time they move. If your children worry that a pet's grave might be disturbed by future residents, you might help them plant a tree over it. With a little thought, you can find ways to help your children bring closure to their relationship with their pet before they move away.

7

Don't be afraid to throw your own goodbye party.

Some of you say, 'Joy is greater than sorrow,' and
others say, 'Nay, sorrow is the greater.' But I say
unto you, they are inseparable. Together they come,
and when one sits alone with you at your board,
remember that the other is asleep upon your bed.

—Kahlil Gibran, *The Prophet*

I'm not going to say goodbye now, because I know I'll see you
again before you leave." I can't tell you how many times I have
heard someone say that, only to have moving day come and go
without seeing them again. My guess is that, in the majority of
these cases, the people are just trying to avoid having to say that
final goodbye.

A few of my friends have admitted that they avoid saying goodbye because they don't want their children to see them cry, or they
can't stand to see their children cry. Why would we want to give the
message to our children that it's not okay to cry when you're sad?
There are probably at least 50 children and adults in seven states
who have seen me cry when saying goodbye, and I don't think any
of them have been emotionally scarred by the experience.
Goodbyes *are* painful, but the closure that comes with a goodbye is
a necessary part of moving on.

I believe that a goodbye party is to moving what a funeral or memorial service is to death. A funeral allows survivors to honor the significance of their relationship with the deceased and to begin the process of emotional healing. Funerals are generally bittersweet: Along with great sadness at the passing of a loved one is joy in remembering all the good times, as well as enjoyment in being reunited with relatives and long-time friends. Goodbye parties, likewise, allow attendees to formally recognize the loss they are about to experience, while at the same time remembering all the happy times they have shared. At every goodbye party I've attended, the heavy feeling of sadness and loss was paralleled with joy at being able to create one last loving memory with dear friends.

If your children's friends or your own friends host a goodbye party for your family, sit back and enjoy their labor of love. But if no one volunteers to give a goodbye party for your children, then—with apologies to Miss Manners—just throw one for them yourself. Let your children determine what type of party it should be. Besides an agreed-upon budget, the only rule I provide for my kids is that planning and preparations have to be simple; the last thing I want to do when we're about to move is add a complicated project to my long to-do list. Sometimes my children have decided to invite two or three of their best friends over for pizza or a sleepover. Other times they have wanted to involve their whole class or a large group of friends. In both Topeka and Baltimore, we held very successful goodbye parties at community swimming pools. The preparations consisted simply of making invitations and providing store-bought drinks and light refreshments. My children invited as many friends as they wanted, and their friends' families were welcome to stay. We essentially had three parties in one, with my children playing predominantly with their own friends but also interacting with their siblings' friends, many of whom they had come to know fairly well.

We learned, by trial and error, to specify on the party invitation that guests should not bring gifts. We want the children in attendance to enjoy the party without any strings attached. Besides, if gifts are received then sending thank-you notes is another item to add to that long to-do list (a great alternative to gift-giving is discussed in the next chapter).

Probably the most memorable goodbye celebration we've had was an impromptu "empty house" party. It was the first time we moved with the kids, from Louisville, Kentucky. Our children were young (ages five years, three years, and eight months), and the neighbors had thrown a block party in our honor several weeks previously. Because of scheduling problems, we had two days after the moving truck left before we could leave town. As we were walking through the incredibly lonely house with all our possessions gone, it occurred to us that the empty house would be a great spot for a party—especially for families with a lot of little kids. We quickly spread the word (which was easy to do in our tightly knit cul-de-sac community), and at 7:00 that evening neighbors began flowing in, with folding chairs, coolers, and whatever snacks they happened to have in their pantries. As you can imagine, the preschoolers had a blast running around (and around, and around) the empty house, and the adults enjoyed a relaxing, effortless get-together.

The empty-house party was a wonderful, spontaneous way to have one more evening of fun and laughter with our friends. But, more important, it created a lasting memory in our minds: When we picture our empty house in Louisville, we don't see vacant, lonely rooms. Rather, we see laughing children and happy adults, celebrating friendship.

> "One thing my parents do to help make moving easier is let us have a going-away party. It's fun to get to play with our friends for the last time before we move away. My parents always ask the people who are coming to bring a letter they have written so we can remember them."
>
> MARK, AGE 10

Of course, sometimes it isn't practical to host a goodbye party, even a very informal one. After Connie's marriage dissolved, her children had only a week to say goodbye to their friends. Because this didn't allow time for planning a party, Connie made sure her sons took time from the work of packing and cleaning to visit and formally say goodbye to all their friends. On moving day, many of these friends showed up to help the family finish packing and load the van—a demonstration of friendship that meant a lot to Connie's sons.

If your children will be leaving behind an adult who has played a large role in their lives, such as a parent (if you are divorcing), a grandparent, or a long-time nanny or teacher, make sure each child has some private time to say his or her goodbyes. This person might also participate in the goodbye party, of course, but your child needs one-on-one time to express his or her feelings and to discuss specific ways in which they will maintain their relationship after the move.

Finally, don't forget the importance of saying goodbye to some of the places that have been important in your child's life. A young child may want to actually wave bye-bye to the preschool, the babysitter's house, the playground, and other favorite places. Now that my children are older, before we move we make final trips to our favorite ice-cream store, restaurant, and park, and to other special places we have frequented to savor the memories one last time.

Before we are ready to embrace the new opportunities waiting for us after the move, we need to say a formal goodbye to those people and places that will soon become an important part of our past. Whether you plan a small gathering of close friends, a large pool party, an empty-house party, a round of short visits to friends' houses, or another event of your choosing, make sure your children have the opportunity to bring closure to the everyday relationships they are leaving behind, while celebrating the experiences they have shared with these friends—experiences that will enrich their lives forever.

8

Take tangible keepsakes with you.

Dear Rebecca, I hope you have a wonderful time in Kanses. Tommrow you won't be a table washer because you have moved. I will be the only one to clean the chairs and wash the table. I will miss you a lot. I can't tickle you anymore! I can't call you because you won't be there. How long will you be there? Will you ever meet me again? Love, Charlie
—Letter from my daughter Rebecca's friend Charlie, second grade

When my oldest child, Rebecca, started talking, a good friend of mine, whose second child was Rebecca's age, instructed, "Lori, you need to write down all those cute things Becca says so you don't forget them." Several years later, I thanked my friend for suggesting such a great way to help me preserve all those memories—I was surprised how quickly I could forget the important details. My friend grinned and replied, "Yeah, I really need to do that myself."

Memories do fade. It's important to have keepsakes of the people and the memories we cherish, both to help us remember past experiences and to provide comfort and warmth when we are missing those people and the times we shared with them. Ensuring that your children have one or more keepsakes to take with them when they move will help ease the transition by providing a link between their past identity and their identity in their new home. Some children may want to place their keepsake where they can see it every day, whereas others may want to bring it out only when they're in the right mood to ponder the memories it provokes.

Some parents fear that having a tangible memory of the past may encourage children to dwell on what they left behind rather than concentrate on the present. I haven't found this to be a problem; rather, my children seem to turn to their keepsakes when they need some comfort or a boost of self-confidence. But if you find that your child is relying on a keepsake instead of making new friends, ask your child about how things are going and what you can do to help with the transition.

Use your creativity to find keepsakes that match your child's personality and your family's circumstances. Married to a career military officer, Laurie knew when they began their family that her children would spend their childhoods moving from place to place. So she began a "Friends Scrapbook" for Matthew and Megan. The scrapbook is filled with pictures of friends who have been special to Laurie's children in every place they have lived. Pictures of them with their guinea pig and bunny in Germany are in the scrapbook, too. Her older child, Matthew, particularly likes to spend time looking at the scrapbook, remembering the friends he has had over the past 10 years.

Another creative military mom, Lisa, has created a variety of meaningful keepsakes for her children when they have moved. She held one of her son's going-away parties at a make-your-own-pottery center. Each guest put his thumbprint and signature on a piece of pottery for her son to keep. Lisa always brings a T-shirt to her children's going-away parties and ensures that their friends sign it before they leave. When her sons are grown, Lisa plans to make the signed T-shirts into a quilt. Lisa also has the guests write their names with fabric paint on the tablecloth at every birthday party, so her children can look back years later and see who their friends were at each age.

> "There is one thing that my parents never did that would make moving easier. A great idea would be to take a picture of each room in the old house, fully furnished, before you start packing. That would be one way to remember the old house and to preserve all of the great memories."
>
> SARAH, AGE 13

When my daughter Sarah was in fifth grade, she and three other girls were close friends. When we found out that one of the foursome was going to move, Sarah hosted a going-away slumber party. I found unpainted ceramic signs that said Friends, in raised letters, at a discount store, and I bought one for each of the four girls. They spent a good part of the evening painting the signs and writing personal messages on the back. Each girl left the party with a tangible keepsake.

The idea for my family's favorite type of keepsake came from Mrs. Petrea, Rebecca's thoughtful second-grade teacher. On Becca's last day of school in Atlanta, Mrs. Petrea presented her with a memory book that included a letter from each child in her class, as well as photos of Becca and her friends throughout the school year. In subsequent moves, we have asked each friend coming to the goodbye party to bring a letter, complete with address and phone number, to put in a three-ring binder. When we hold a combined party, we

IDEAS FOR MEANINGFUL KEEPSAKES

Memory book with letters from friends

Collage of pictures and mementos of significant events

T-shirt signed by friends

Clay plaque with friends' names and thumbprints

Photo album with pictures of friends

Video or picture album of your house and other special places

Video with individual messages from friends

Signed ball from teammates

Christmas ornament or refrigerator magnet with pictures of
    special people

Framed group picture

make sure that friends provide separate letters for Becca, Sarah, and Mark so that they can each put one in a memory book. As I was preparing to write this chapter, I asked my children to show me their memory books. All three of them knew exactly where their books were and brought them to me in less than a minute. Keep in mind that Becca's second-grade book was eight years and three moves ago!

For younger children, a memory book can be filled with friends' drawings and with letters they have dictated to their parents. By first or second grade, children begin to enjoy writing the letters themselves:

> **"If you like to play catch with your friend, ask him to sign the baseball you usually play with and let you keep it when you move."**
>
> GEORDAN, AGE 10

Mark, Sorry you're moving to Florida. I hope you have a nice teacher. I don't think you will have a mean teacher. I think you will swim every day unless it is raining. Then you might play a game inside. What will you play if you played a game inside? I wrote this by myself on the computer. Your friend, Doug (first grade)

Becca, I feel sad that you are moving. You have neat handwriting. I hope you make new friends. We will all miss you. You were the nicest girl in the class! Love, Michael (second grade)

Friends can do an awesome job of offering encouragement to help ease the fear that comes with a new situation:

Dear Sarah, Thank you so much for being my friend. I am glad you spent a lot of time with me. But I am really sad that you're leaving. I hope your new friends are nice like you were to me. Carla (fourth grade)

Not only do these letters provide warm memories for the child who is moving, but they also help the letter writers come to terms with the loss they are about to experience. This can be seen in the letter from Charlie at the opening of this chapter; you can sense that as he is writing he suddenly realizes that he may never see Rebecca again. The following excerpt shows another one of Becca's friends working through her loss:

You made me laugh, and now that it is time for you to move, I will always laugh because of you. You brought joy into my life and I won't forget the way, that when you laughed, how your nose scrunched up with that one freckle in that weird way. It always seemed that you would never leave but now that you are, I don't want you to go. I'll always remember you in my mind and in my heart. Thanks for being a great friend . . . always. Ashley (sixth grade)

Don't forget to ask for letters from your children's favorite teachers, coaches, and adult neighbors. Rebecca always loved the cookies and other baked goods that the mother of one of her friends made, so the mom filled a memory book page with all of her special recipes. But Becca's favorite memory-book entry is from fun-loving Mr. Stimmel, her first band director, who ignited her passion for music; it puts her in an immediate good mood every time she reads it:

I have this very distinct memory of an incredibly quiet flute class. If only I would have left it there, but no, I had to say, "This class is too quiet." What was I thinking? Couldn't I realize the potential? NO! Because I had yet to see the amazing Becca in action. She dances, she cheers, she flies through the air . . . and that class was quiet no more.

9

Recognize the importance of your child's personal belongings.

When I was sick and lay a-bed,
I had two pillows at my head,
And all my toys beside me lay
to keep me happy all the day.
—Robert Louis Stevenson,
"The Land of Counterpane"

Most young children have a favorite comfort item. You know, the kind that, if lost in the middle of the night, must be found before anyone can get back to sleep. It may be a blanket, a stuffed animal, or a special toy. Or it may be something slightly embarrassing; a two-year-old boy I saw at a daycare center carried a piece of his mother's lingerie with him wherever he went. Mark's favorite item, from the age of two to the age of four, was his black Tasmanian Devil baseball cap. For only two occasions would Mark remove his cap—to take a shower and to have a family picture taken by a professional photographer. The cap was the last thing Mark would remove before his shower and the first thing he would put on when the shower was over. We have pictures of him sleeping in his cap.

I don't remember exactly when Mark decided he didn't need his cap anymore. It may have been as we prepared him for kindergarten, where he would have to adhere to the class's no-hats rule.

Until then, the cap served as a source of comfort for Mark, particularly when Randy and I weren't around. A treasured belonging like Mark's cap is called a security object because a child's attachment to it helps him learn the skill of self-comfort, a valuable coping mechanism for him as he grows up.

During a move, it is important to recognize that your children's personal belongings may be a source of security and comfort for them as they leave beloved people and familiar places behind. Watching these items being packed into a box, the box carried into a truck, and the truck driven out of sight can be stressful. Young children may not understand that their belongings will show up again at their new home. To reduce this stress, there are things parents can do before and after the move to help kids keep track of the items that are important to them.

> "We went from a 2,500-square-foot house to a 1,200-square-foot one, so trying to get the boys' rooms set up in ways similar to what they had been was difficult. But I wanted to make sure that when they walked into their rooms they would see familiar things— the same comforters on their beds, the same toys on their shelves."
>
> CONNIE, SINGLE MOTHER OF FOUR BOYS

As you begin packing your family's belongings, assign each child a backpack to keep close at hand during the move. Help each child as necessary in deciding what to put in the backpack. Encourage your children to pack both things they will use to entertain themselves during the trip and things that they simply don't want to be without until the moving truck arrives. They may want to pack their favorite stuffed animals, dolls, or trucks; a photo album or letters from friends; books, trophies, videotapes, or DVDs; a Game Boy; a music player; or a card or coin collection. When we travel by plane, the only stipulations we put on our kids' packing are that the items they choose have to fit in the zipped backpack and (now that the children are old enough) that the backpacks have to be light enough that the children can carry them through the airport.

Once the first-priority possessions are safely packed in backpacks, let your children decide what their second-priority items are—those items they want to have access to as soon as the moving truck arrives at your new home. If you will have enough space in the moving truck, it's helpful for each child to get one box to fill with second-priority items. Younger children may enjoy decorating their boxes with crayons, paint, or stickers. Make sure each box is clearly labeled with the child's name, and put the boxes in a room full of things that the movers will load last and unload first.

Military families moving overseas are generally allocated a number of pounds for "express shipment" or "hold baggage." This allows the families immediate access to necessities such as linens, towels, and cleaning supplies. Try to include within this limit a few items that will help each child feel at home on arrival, or ship such items ahead. During one move, Laurie left her family's pots and pans out of the hold baggage so that her daughter's prized dollhouse could be included. When moving back to the United States from Germany, Laurie separately shipped a box of her daughter's dolls to her mother's house so that they would be waiting for her daughter when the family arrived.

On moving day, pay attention to how your children are feeling as their boxes are being loaded into the moving truck. Remind younger children that their belongings will be safely transported to their new home. Be flexible; if at the last minute your child is having a hard time parting with a particular item, let her keep it with her if at all possible, even if it isn't something she originally wanted in her backpack.

> "When we get to a new house, I feel better once my bed is ready and my room is all put together. That is one of the first things my parents do to make me feel better."
>
> MEGAN, AGE 7

As soon as the trip is over and the moving boxes have arrived, help your children unpack their specially marked boxes. Resist the temptation to unpack kitchen items first. You might even forget about cooking for a few nights, and instead order pizza or other carryout food to allow more time for helping your children get settled. Lisa, a military mom, puts plenty of paper plates, cups, and plastic utensils in her express shipment so she can focus on her kids' bedrooms without having to look through the kitchen boxes to find essentials for a quick meal.

When setting up the kids' rooms, it is important to keep a balance of old and new. Part of the excitement of a move is the change to new surroundings, so let the kids share in that excitement by changing some of the features of their rooms if they want to. My kids always enjoy picking new comforters, sheets, curtains, and maybe a few wall hangings. Becca and Mark each enjoy picking the paint color for their rooms. Remember, paint doesn't have to be permanent. After my only move as a child, my parents let me paint my bedroom fluorescent yellow and pick out yellow shag carpeting; my brother chose fluorescent green. Wow! I didn't realize what a gift that was until I had a home of my own.

Although a requirement of military housing is that you leave it in the same condition as you found it, Lisa still paints bedroom walls for her children if she thinks that will help them feel more ownership of their new surroundings. She allocates time before the next move to repaint the walls in the same neutral color in which she found them.

The anticipation of being close to the Disney theme parks made Laurie's kids eager to move to Florida. During trips to Disney World and MGM Studios shortly after their move, Laurie and her husband took pictures of their daughter, Megan, with the Disney princesses and their son, Matthew, with Star Wars characters. Then they surprised Megan and Matthew by framing the pictures and decorating their rooms with the Disney princesses and Star Wars themes.

The excitement of new things in the kids' rooms should be supplemented with familiar belongings from their previous home. Make sure their favorite books are on the shelves, their favorite stuffed animals and dolls are there, and pictures of their friends and family are scattered around. The comfort of these ties to the past is as important as the anticipation of new things to come.

Once their rooms are organized, you can tackle the kitchen and other parts of the house while the children are nesting. Exploring their new environment and getting reacquainted with their belongings generally occupies our kids for several days—long enough for us to unpack most of the remaining boxes. Just be sure not to become so involved with unpacking and arranging things that you miss cues from your kids that they need help adjusting. When they start to get bored, or lonely, or sad, just stop what you are doing. Take them for a walk through the neighborhood to scope out kids their age. Or take time to talk. Or play. Or laugh. Or cry. Just make sure your kids know that they are the most important valuables in your imaginary first-priority backpack.

10

Use the move as a chance to reorganize.

Organization is as important to older children as routine is to younger ones.

Organization is one of my strengths. Before you accuse me of bragging, let me point out that I recognize the fine line between being highly organized and being compulsive about it. I think I generally stay on the side of healthy organizational efforts, but I did wonder when I discovered that a boss was hiding brochures about time-management seminars from me.

Perhaps I'm an overzealous organizer sometimes. All the same, teaching your children organizational skills can help foster their sense of confidence and order, and it can provide a framework for success in school and throughout life. We have been told by experts for years how important routine is to small children. Similarly, organizational skills can help older children avoid being overwhelmed with too much information or too many activities. This is particularly important in the midst of the chaos that typically surrounds a move.

In the four-year period in which our family lived in four different states, I estimate that we had a house on the market 25 percent of the time. For a total of one year, then, we had to have the house clean enough that it could be shown to a prospective buyer with as little as 30 minutes' notice. And, every time we left the house, it had to be presentable in case a real-estate agent stopped by while we were out. Although this created a great deal of stress in our lives, my children learned that it truly is easier to keep one's room clean and one's personal items in order than to do a big cleaning once a week. (Well, actually only two of my three children believe this. The third seems to function better when she has clothes lying on the floor and personal items thrown haphazardly around her bedroom.) My house, except for Becca's room, is clutter-free. And this is not because I bug my kids to keep it that way. We just have found that we save time and reduce stress by keeping our items well organized. Many other families who move frequently have learned to be just as tidy.

> "My kids have become very well organized because we have moved so much. Our philosophy is that if you're not using it, you should get rid of it. I think the hardest thing for me to do when we stop moving will be to continue to get rid of the clutter."
>
> LAURIE,
> MOTHER OF TWO

Moving provides a wonderful opportunity to talk with your children about the importance of organizational skills. Enlist their help in implementing the following organizational steps:

1. **Develop a to-do list.** Write down all the tasks that need to be accomplished during the move, and then put them in order of priority. Note the date by which each task must be accomplished. Assign a person to be responsible for completing each task, and then hold that person accountable. When you complete a task, cross it off the list, in red ink. This allows the kids to see the progress you are all making.

2. **Get rid of your clutter.** Moving is the perfect time to get rid of the toys, clothes, furniture, and knickknacks that you no longer use. I let my children have a garage sale each time we move. They are responsible for choosing which of their belongings they want to sell, pricing them (with some guidance from me), and then being on

hand to sell them the day of the sale. We agree on two conditions: They get to keep the money they get from selling their belongings (depending on how much they make, some of the money may go into their savings accounts) and, once an item is in the garage ready to be sold, it's not allowed back into the house. In other words, if it doesn't sell, it gets donated to charity.

K.C., a stay-at-home dad, let his kids hold a garage sale when the family moved from Baltimore to New Jersey. He was amused at how many toys his children were willing to part with when they knew the proceeds could be used to buy new toys for their new home.

When I'm unloading boxes after a move, I always find more things we don't need. I keep two extra boxes in each room: one labeled "Charitable Donations" and one labeled "Trash." The more boxes I unpack, the more eager I am to give away something that we rarely use. We have become so accustomed to getting rid of our clutter that we now make two or three donations of gently used items each year to a local charity.

3. **Organize small items in small containers.** After spending countless hours during the first couple of moves unwrapping yards of paper to find one Barbie doll shoe or two pencils, I decided I could save myself much time if I organized small items, such as school supplies and toys, before a move; these items actually now stay somewhat organized in small containers throughout the year. (We still haven't figured out whether it was a quirky sense of humor or a mean streak that possessed our movers to place a key piece of a board game at the bottom of one of our kitchen boxes and a pair of Barbie shoes in my clothes box!)

4. **Let your children develop their own organizational systems.** Some people can function in the midst of clutter better than others can. If it is important to your child to keep old letters and papers, don't insist that he throw them away for the sake of organization. Agree that he can keep them as long as they are placed in a drawer, box, or some place besides his bedroom floor.

5. **Continually reassess what's important.** Review your prioritized checklist regularly. If important tasks have taken longer to complete than
you planned, determine which items can be deleted from the list,
where shortcuts can be taken, or which tasks can be postponed.
Distinguish the tasks that you really have to do from the ones you
want to do and the ones you'll do only if you have time. Let your
children help you prioritize items that will affect them. For example,
if you don't have time both to make cookies for your daughter's last
dance class and to call around to find a new dance class in the
community to which you're moving, ask your daughter which is more
important to her.

6. **Break large projects into small tasks.** This organizational skill will help
your child tremendously in life. The idea of a month-long project is
generally too daunting for a child. Teach her to determine what
tasks need to be done each day so that the project will be completed on time, and help her develop the discipline to complete the
necessary tasks each day. Don't show her through example the
stress that results from trying to pack a whole house in one day.

7. **Maintain a sense of balance.** Leave time for relaxation. Once you and
your children complete a task, reward yourselves by doing something fun.

8. **Politely say no.** Understand your limits. Spreading yourself too thin,
particularly during a move, is doing a disservice to yourself and
your children. Demonstrate assertiveness and self-respect by saying no to other commitments. As children move into their teen
years, the ability to say no politely yet assertively will prove invaluable to them.

By teaching organizational skills to your children, you can help
them create order out of chaos. This will reduce the stress they feel
and give them a sense of control in their lives.

11

Make the move an adventure.

O beautiful for spacious skies, for amber waves of grain,
For purple mountain majesties above the fruited plain!
America! America! God shed His grace on thee.
—Katharine Lee Bates, "America the Beautiful"

As you conduct research related to your move, you might buy a map of your new city or town and pick up a directory from the local phone company. Plot on the map your new home, school, parks, libraries, stores, places of worship, and other sites of interest. This will help your children visualize their new community. Put the map on the wall, so the kids can study it at their leisure.

Gather information on special places to visit as well. Call or visit the local Visitors' Bureau or Chamber of Commerce to get pamphlets and flyers about the area and about its kid-friendly attractions. Look both for attractions similar to your kids' favorites in your present town (for example, a skating rink, a water park, tennis courts, an outdoor market) and for attractions unlike any found where you live now. Plotting these on the map and talking about them with the children will help create both a sense of familiarity and a sense of excitement about new adventures.

If you have the opportunity to visit the new area with your children before you move, make sure you devote time to exploring. Take the map on which you plotted the points of interest, and go on a "treasure hunt" to find each landmark. As you walk through your new neighborhood, look for bikes, basketball hoops, trampolines, and other play equipment in driveways and backyards. If neighbors are outside, be sure to introduce yourself and your children and tell them when you'll be moving in. Take a tour of the new school, including the classrooms, cafeteria, playground, gym, and bathrooms. Pick up a snack at the local store and eat it in the neighborhood park, or have lunch in a local restaurant.

If it's impossible to take your children with you to the new area before you move, then take pictures or make a video recording for them of the house, neighborhood, and some key points of interest. If you are moving overseas, have pictures sent to you.

If you do take your children on a pre-move trip, try to allow enough time for a visit to an attraction that makes your new community special. When we made our pre-move trip with the children to Tampa, a visit to Disney's Magic Kingdom was an easy way to build excitement about moving to Florida. Likewise, Baltimore's Inner Harbor and Atlanta's Stone Mountain Park are one-of-a-kind attractions that immediately showed our children something special about their new home. Granted, some areas more easily generate excitement than others. But it didn't take much research into Topeka, Kansas, to discover Gage Park and the Topeka Zoo, where we came face to face with gorillas, enjoyed one of America's few original carousels still in operation, and rode the mini-train around the park. Had our children been older, a trip to Worlds of Fun theme park in Kansas City would have been a good option.

Once moving day has arrived, you can even make the drive or plane journey fun. In this age of Game Boys and in-car DVD players, it is tempting to let the kids fill all the long hours of a moving trip with electronic entertainment (don't forget the batteries!). If you exercise your creativity, though, you'll find ways to make the trip an adventure. The kids should have some of their favorite games and toys already packed securely in their backpacks; surprise them with some new games, too, such as Outburst, Password, or Mad Libs. Bring along one of the many books of travel activities for kids. My family has spent countless hours playing highway scavenger hunts (looking for three license plates from Indiana or two drivers with comb-overs), the alphabet game (finding a sign with a word starting with *A*, then *B*, *C*, and so on), and the first-last letter game (naming an item in a category, such as food, then naming another item in the category that begins with the last letter of the previous item—for example, steak, ketchup, peach, hamburger, and so on). One travel book we bought had a list of thought-provoking questions that helped us get to know each other better (for example, "If you could spend the day with one person who has died, who would it be and why?" "If a magical genie granted you three wishes, what would you wish?" "Tell us about your most embarrassing moment."). If you are crossing state lines, look for license plates from the destination state. Discuss the significance of what's on the plates, such as the leaping salmon on some Oregon plates or New Hampshire's motto, Live Free or Die. Sing together, especially silly songs, or sing in harmony if the kids are musical. Listen to recorded stories. At highway rest stops, have a picnic, throw around a flying disc or ball, gather tourism pamphlets, or explore the local flora. Or take breaks at truck stops and curious-looking highway restaurants. Take advantage of your captive audience and delight in the opportunity for family bonding.

> "Living in six different places has helped me know that when you first get somewhere, you should just start to explore. In Maryland, we lived in front of a large golf course and next to hilly woods. My brother, sister, and I explored the woods and got to know it like it was our house. We built forts and discovered nice relaxing areas and places to climb, and we even had a rope to swing across the small stream that ran through the woods. That is how we met our new neighbors, and we still are friends today."
>
> SARAH, AGE 13

Understanding how quickly children get bored during long trips, Lisa has developed a wonderful travel gift that she presents to friends who are moving. She buys a shower-caddy box or small bucket and fills it with her friends' favorite snacks, games for the trip (cards, word-search puzzles), an address book with her children's address written in, and—if she can find it on the Internet—a list of "silly facts" about the place to which they are moving.

IDEAS FOR MAKING YOUR MOVE AN ADVENTURE

BEFORE THE MOVE

Get a map of your new community and plot points of interest.

Call or visit the Chamber of Commerce or Visitors' Bureau and ask for pamphlets about local and regional attractions.

Search the Internet for information on local events and customs.

Make a pre-move visit to tour the schools and other points of interest.

DURING THE MOVING TRIP

Bring a small bag for each child with special snacks and treats.

Surprise the kids with a new game, such as Outburst or Password.

Play car games such as the alphabet game and I-spy.

Let the kids guess answers to questions about their new city or state.

AFTER THE MOVE

Let the kids make a city out of boxes in an empty room while you're unpacking.

Have a contest to see who can collect the most mover's stickers or find a specially marked box.

Take a walk through your neighborhood and see who can be the first to strike up a conversation with a neighbor.

Spend weekends and holidays exploring unique places surrounding your new home.

Even though there is much work to be done when you arrive at your new home, there are ways to make the unpacking fun for your kids. Put a gold star on one of the packed boxes before you move, and then challenge your kids to find it. You might even place an inexpensive, wrapped present for each child inside the box, and let the kids open their gifts when they find the specially marked box. When you have unpacked boxes of various sizes, let your kids make a box city in the empty dining room.

Once you have settled in, keep that sense of adventure alive! Have you noticed that many people who have lived in a community for a long time never visit the special sites that attract visitors from long distances? Don't take for granted the special offerings of your community. Use your weekends, summers, and holidays to explore historical, educational, and entertaining places surrounding your new home. While living in Atlanta, the kids and I discovered Helen, Georgia, a re-creation of an Alpine village nestled in the Blue Ridge Mountains. We spent several weekends exploring this quaint town when Randy had to be away for work. When we lived in Topeka, the kids and I read Laura Ingalls Wilder's Little House books and then took a day trip to Independence, Kansas, to visit the official Little House on the Prairie historical site. Of course, some of my friends thought I was a little crazy to drive three hours each way with three young children to visit a site that took us, at most, one and a half hours to explore, but we considered the car ride part of the adventure. Living in Baltimore was an explorer's dream, because of the proximity to other cities. We visited Washington, D.C.; New York City; Philadelphia; Boston; Mystic, Connecticut; and Virginia Beach.

I remember driving with the kids on a back road in Topeka on a

> "When I moved to Maryland, I got to go to the Inner Harbor. We were also close enough to go to New York City and Boston, where I went to the Boston Tea Party ship. When I lived in Kansas, I went to San Antonio on my spring break, and while I was there I visited the Alamo, where I learned about the Mexican-American battle. I also went to the house where Laura Ingalls lived in *Little House on the Prairie*."
>
> MARK, AGE 10

beautiful, sunny morning, admiring the large wheat stalks blowing in the wind, when it suddenly dawned on me what Katharine Lee Bates was envisioning when she wrote, "O beautiful for spacious skies, for amber waves of grain." I had repeated that phrase at least 100 times without ever really thinking about what it meant. That morning, I appreciated for the first time that, though it lacks the awe-inspiring ocean scenery of Florida and the majestic mountain views of Georgia and Maryland, Kansas indeed has a special beauty all its own.

Every place in the world has something that makes it special; you just have to take the time to notice it. Before and after your move, help your children discover the adventure and beauty that is unique to your new home. When you discover your area's special qualities, you begin to develop a sense of community pride and belonging. I'll talk about this concept in greater detail in chapter 17.

12

Support your children as they mourn the loss of loved ones.

*The bitterest thing in our today's sorrow
is the memory of our yesterday's joy.*

—Kahlil Gibran, *Sand and Foam*

There is no getting around it: Moving brings with it pain and sadness. Even if your children are excited about the move, they probably feel some sadness, anxiety, and fear at leaving behind familiar people, places, and routines. If moving means separating from a parent, grandparent, best friend, caregiver, pet, or anyone else with whom your children have had a significant relationship, the loss will likely invoke real grief. Many kids seem to have a natural resilience that helps them bounce back after a disappointment. It is important, however, not to underestimate how difficult the loss may be for your kids.

One of the hardest parts of moving is leaving friends. True friendships, nurtured properly, can withstand the test of time and distance, but the comfortable, everyday relationships with friends who live nearby cease to exist when you move. As I told one of my best friends before I moved 1,100 miles away, "We'll always have the type of friendship that will let us pick up where we left off." But

I miss being able to say to her, "Boy, I had a rough day. Let's sit down and drink a couple of Diet Dr Peppers and commiserate." As painful as it is for adults to leave friends behind, the sadness may be even greater for children. A child may be used to seeing her best friend every day. The two children may see no future for their relationship, especially if they can't yet read or write. Each may wonder whether she'll ever have another best friend.

When a move occurs as a result of a divorce or a parent's death, the loss of the parent's presence compounds the stress of other losses. Even if a failing marriage has caused a lot of tension in your home, or a long-term illness has drained the family's energy, the relief that follows a death or divorce will likely be secondary to the sadness your children must feel. During the aftermath, it will be important for your children to have keepsakes to connect them to their missing parent, and, in the case of divorce, to ensure there is frequent communication with the parent they had to leave behind.

During and after her divorce, Connie knew it was important not to say negative things about her boys' father and to encourage their relationship with him. If one of her boys was missing his dad and wanted to telephone him, she made sure that happened. By ensuring that her boys maintained regular phone contact with their dad and by making a six-hour drive so they could visit him once a month, she helped them feel more connected to him. She also made sure to maintain a relationship with her sons' relatives on their dad's side, by hosting them for visits a couple of times a year.

For some children, leaving a grandparent can be nearly as hard as leaving a parent. When K.C.'s family moved from Chicago to Baltimore, his children had never before lived more than a few miles away from their grandparents. Because K.C. knew this would be a hard transition, he arranged to have the grandparents visit just a couple of weeks after the move. This helped his children understand that, even though Grandma and Grandpa now lived far away, the family would still be able to maintain regular contact with them. K.C. and his wife also kept the grandparents updated on all of the kids' milestones and successes, which allowed the grandparents to call and share in the children's joys when they couldn't celebrate together in person.

Although you cannot take away the pain of separation from your children, there are several things you can do to help make the pain more bearable. Encourage your kids to express how they are feeling, and never judge what they tell you. Saying things like "Don't worry, you'll make new friends," or "Don't feel sad," would give them the message that their feelings are unacceptable. Be honest about how *you* are feeling, too; if you are sad, say so. And don't impose a time limit on your children's grief—let them feel each emotion for as long as they need to feel it.

In her book *On Death and Dying* (Scribner, 1997), Elisabeth Kübler-Ross identifies five stages of grief: denial-isolation, anger, bargaining, depression, and, finally, acceptance. These emotions are experienced in varying degrees not only after a death but after any major loss—divorce, unemployment, the emptying of a nest as children grow up, and a move away from family and friends. In the case of a move, the grieving can begin during the planning phase. If you understand how the stages of grief can play out, you will be better able to support your children through their mourning.

> "Missing your friends is usually the worst thing for me. I can hardly say goodbye sometimes. Sometimes after I've moved, I wake up and say, 'I think I'll go to *whoever's* house today,' but then I remember I can't because I'm gone. That makes me feel really sad."
>
> MARK, AGE 10

As you read the following paragraphs, keep in mind that the process of grieving can vary a lot. There is no right or wrong way to grieve. You and your children may skip some stages or go through all of them in a different order than usual. Or maybe your children won't grieve at all during or after a move; they may be glad to leave a place where they haven't been happy.

During the stage of denial and isolation, children may try to convince themselves that Mom and Dad will change their minds, that the new job offer will fall through, or that something else will happen to prevent the move or cause the family to move back to their old home. One of my friends discovered that her daughter was trying to sabotage the sale of their house by messing up rooms that her mom had just cleaned for a showing; the girl assumed that if the house didn't sell, then the family couldn't move. I still carry in my memory the vivid, haunting picture of my daughter, who rarely cries when she is upset, bursting into tears and screaming, "No, we can't move again, we just can't!" Often, children in denial will isolate themselves and will refuse to respond to their parents' efforts at consolation. Their despair at the thought of giving up everything they know is overwhelming.

Often hardest for parents to tolerate is the anger stage. Parents naturally comfort a child who is sad and despondent, but their patience may quickly dissipate when the child starts lashing out. The key to helping a child through this stage is to let him feel safe expressing his anger in appropriate ways. Tell your child that it's okay for him to tell you that he's mad at you, to hit a punching bag or pillow, to play his heart out on the soccer field or basketball court, or to write in his journal about how unfair life is. But it's not okay for him to hit his little brother, to tear up the For Sale sign in the front yard, or to stay out after curfew. Please don't ask your child to ignore the anger he feels inside or imply that there's something wrong with it. Anger is a natural reaction. Your child needs to know that you love him and will stand by him even when he is feeling his angriest. Like denial and isolation, anger can appear before or after the move or both. The anger may dissipate and then return, especially if the child doesn't make new friends right away.

> "When I'd call my dad after we moved away, sometimes I would feel a little bit better, but sometimes it would make me miss him more. I missed having him read to me and be there when I went to bed."
>
> GEORDAN, AGE 10

Once the anger begins to subside, children sometimes enter a bargaining stage. They may try to convince you why you shouldn't move, or why you should move back. They may promise they'll get better grades or help out more around the house or be nicer to their siblings, if only they don't have to move. An older child may offer to get a part-time job to make up for the salary increase that would come with a parent's job promotion.

The sadness children feel during the depression stage of grief can be heart-wrenching for a parent to witness. Some children are aware that their sadness is related to the move; others don't know why they feel as they do. My children sometimes express their sadness by crying more easily at trivial matters and generally acting more irritable and cranky. I try to help them get in touch with their feelings without imposing my own feelings on them. This is difficult. I might say, "I noticed that you snapped at your sister several times today when she was trying to help you; let's talk about what's going on." Or, "When I walked by your room, I heard you crying. Can we talk about what's making you feel so sad?" Children are often most willing to talk about their feelings at bedtime—when they're tired and their defenses are down.

As in the anger stage, you can help children through the depres-

WAYS TO HELP YOUR CHILDREN DEAL WITH GRIEF

Understand that there is no right or wrong way to grieve.

Encourage your children to express how they are feeling.

Listen to them, and don't judge or minimize their feelings.

Be honest about your own feelings.

Don't impose a time limit on your children's grief.

Help your children find appropriate ways to express anger and sadness.

Show them, through example, the importance of carrying on regular school, work, and home activities while grieving.

Seek professional help if you see signs of a serious problem.

Offer unconditional love at all times.

sion stage by letting them know their feelings are perfectly normal, comforting them when they'll let you, and offering unconditional love at all times. Don't minimize their feelings by telling them that "everything will be okay, so snap out of it." Everything *will* be okay, of course, but children need to feel safe expressing their innermost emotions. When they are crying because they are missing their friends, you might say, "I miss my friends, too. That sadness really hurts, doesn't it?" Or, if you can't find the words to comfort them, just hold them and tell them that you're sorry they're sad and that you love them.

Children generally get their cues from their parents. Kids who observe their parents expressing anger and sadness in appropriate, healthy ways learn to cope in similar ways. It's okay to tell your children that you are sad and lonely. In fact, pretending that you're not sad and lonely is a bad idea. You can't expect your children to be comfortable expressing their feelings if you are trying to hide yours. Knowing that their parents can be sad or angry and yet still function at home and at work is a critical lesson for children.

No one can tell you exactly how long the depression or any of the other stages of grief will last for your child. In the relocation workshops provided by the military, according to one military mom, the leaders advise against making judgments about a place until you have lived there six months, because that's generally how long it takes adults to deal with the emotional turmoil of a move. Children may also take this long to work through all the stages of grief.

If you feel that your child's depression is lasting too long or affecting his ability to function, don't be afraid to seek professional help. This is critical if your child stops eating or sleeping well or makes comments about life not being worthwhile. If you think you're seeing signs of a serious problem, trust your instincts and get counseling immediately. If you have moved at your company's request, don't hesitate to ask whether your employer would be willing to pay for this counseling.

With time and adequate parental support, most children will move through denial, anger, bargaining, and depression and into acceptance. They will have learned some valuable lessons:

When we come upon a situation we can't change, we need to accept it and make the most of it.

Even good decisions can have painful consequences.

The love and support of one's family is invaluable.

True friends remain friends no matter how much time and distance separate them.

With the right attitude, there can be joy at the end of sorrow.

Your children's acceptance of a move doesn't mean that their pain and loneliness have gone away completely, or that they won't still miss the friends and places they have left behind. Rather, it means they have chosen not to let the pain paralyze them. They have decided to discover and embrace the new opportunities, friendships, and happiness that are waiting for them on the other side.

13

Take deliberate steps to ease the transition to a new school.

It takes a whole village to raise a child.

—African proverb

At a mall a few years ago, I ran into a woman I had seen at Rebecca's school but had never spoken with. I introduced myself and found out that "Teri" had moved to the community a year before my family had. As we compared notes on our move and our kids' transitions, Teri expressed extreme dissatisfaction with her daughter's first teacher at the school; this teacher, Teri said, had done nothing to help Teri's daughter adjust. In fact, the girl still didn't like the community, and Teri felt that the teacher was at least partially responsible. I told Teri what a shame that was, and that my daughter's first teacher at the same school had been a great help in easing Becca's transition. She had assigned Becca a buddy to sit with in the classroom and at lunch, made sure Becca had the necessary background information on the topics the class was studying, and periodically checked with me to see whether there was anything else she could do to help.

Imagine Teri's and my surprise when we realized we were talking about the same teacher! Teri's daughter had the same teacher as

Rebecca just one year previously, but the girls' experiences had been totally different. With my curiosity piqued, I explored with Teri the question of what could account for the difference in this teacher's behavior with the two girls. Finally I figured it out: I had initiated a conversation with the teacher before Becca went to school the first day, explained that Becca had been through several moves in a short period of time, and asked for the teacher's help in making Becca feel comfortable in her new environment. In contrast, Teri's first discussion with the teacher occurred about six weeks into the school year—long after her daughter had begun to feel alienated and frustrated.

A successful transition to a new school is one of the most important parts of a child's adjustment to a new home. You can help your child by taking deliberate steps to make this transition smooth.

If possible, begin by visiting the school with your children before enrolling them. The first day of class isn't as scary if your kids have toured the school, heard the school rules, and met their teachers in advance. Walk with them through the classrooms, cafeteria, gymnasium, and administrative offices. Ask the tour guide to show them the bathrooms, the playground, and the nurse's office. If your son plays a band instrument, go to the band room and meet the director. If your daughter loves sports, talk with the physical education teacher about the school's athletic program. Make sure you ask about the dress code, extracurricular activities, and transportation.

If it's not possible to visit the school before your children's first day of class, check whether the school has a Web site. If so, explore it with your children, and then call and talk with the principal, the guidance counselor, or a teacher. The more your children know about their school in advance, the more comfortable they will feel during the first days of class.

To avoid an embarrassing or disheartening delay on your children's first day of school, you'll want to ask what documents you'll need to bring to enroll the children, and whether the enrollment forms can be mailed to you so you can fill them out in advance. K.C. learned this lesson the hard way after his family moved to Baltimore. When they arrived at the school on the day his children were to start classes, they were told that they were missing one of the required health records. The kids, already nervous about starting at a new school, felt even more anxious when they realized there was a problem. On a subsequent move to New Jersey, K.C. made sure all the paperwork was completed—and verified— before he brought the kids to school for their first day of class.

For a child in elementary school, or for an older child who faces particular challenges, it helps to talk with the teachers and coach before the child begins attending class or practice. Don't put your child in a situation in which a teacher may misinterpret his shyness as conceit, her learning disability as a lack of intelligence, or his height as a sign that he is older than he is. Describe your child's abilities and needs to the teachers, and offer specific suggestions about how they can help with the transition. Say which subjects are your daughter's strengths and in which subjects she may need a little extra help. Let the band director know that music is your son's passion, and that he will want to know about extra performance opportunities. Ask the soccer coach to introduce your daughter to her new teammates before practice begins (don't assume the coach will automatically do this—Sarah joined a team in mid-season when she was in first grade, and the coach never did officially introduce her to her teammates). In my experience, most teachers and other adults who work with children are more than willing to make an effort to help new children feel welcome, but they may not recognize the need to do this unless a parent points it out to them. If you speak with them before the first day of class or practice, not only will they watch out for your child, but they may also consider in advance how they can make your child more comfortable.

"My mom always talks to my teachers before school starts to inform them that I'm new. That makes it easier on me because then, if the teacher is nice, she'll sit me next to people that she thinks I could be friends with. One of the friends my teacher sat me next to at the beginning of the year when we moved here three years ago is one of my very good friends today."
SARAH, AGE 13

In describing your child's needs, be as specific as possible. For example, Sarah is passionate about sports and wants nothing to do with "girly" things, such as makeup and jewelry. Knowing this, her first teacher in Tampa assigned her a buddy with similar athletic interests. This was important for Sarah, who would have rather eaten lunch alone than have had to sit with a group of girls who were talking about their crushes on boys. Instead, Sarah and her new friend, Jaclyn, enjoyed discussing how they beat the boys in soccer at recess!

As many parents can tell you, the first day of school is one of the most stressful milestones of a move. Randy and I stay home from work on this day so that we can give our kids our undivided attention before and after school. I make sure the kids start the day with their favorite breakfast and that we have some time to chat before they leave for school. As the children return home, Randy and I sit down with them and talk about their day. We spend the evening sharing a nice home-cooked dinner (not hot dogs or macaroni and cheese), which may be followed by a trip to the ice-cream store. Regardless of their age, all three of the children have appreciated this special attention on their first day at a new school.

Once school is under way, some parents find that volunteering at the school helps the children's transition; others, however, find that their children adjust more easily if the parent isn't around. Discuss with your children in advance how involved they would like you to be, and then respect their wishes. When my children were in elementary school, they loved for me to be the room parent. Somewhere between late elementary school and early middle school, however, they went from wanting me in their classrooms and school cafeteria as much as possible to feeling embarrassed by my presence at the school. They still liked me to go on field trips and help at classroom parties, but lunches were out, my attendance at school dances was forbidden, and—heaven forbid—a goodbye kiss was grounds for capital punishment! My high-schooler would prefer never to see me on the school grounds, unless I'm transporting her to an extracurricular activity. Take your cues from your children, and get involved to the extent that their needs and your other commitments allow.

If you aren't volunteering at the school regularly, it is important to maintain regular communication with their teachers in some other way, even if your child is in middle or high school. Attend parent orientations and parent-teacher conferences. If your child is having difficulty in a class, ask the teacher how you can reinforce lessons at home. If your child really enjoys a particular class, thank the teacher for making the class interesting.

If you keep lines of communication with teachers open, you will be ready to deal with problems before they escalate. A teacher or coach who recognizes that a child is feeling isolated may not know how to help the child feel more at ease. You know your children better than anyone. You know what makes them uncomfortable, and you know what others could do to make them feel more comfortable in a new situation. When your child is sick, you do not hesitate to ask a medical professional for help. So if your child's adjustment to a move could be improved with the help of a teacher or another adult, do not hesitate to ask for that help. When Connie and her sons moved after her divorce, she talked with their new teachers about the circumstances surrounding their move. When one of her sons was experiencing a particularly difficult challenge, his favorite teacher immediately contacted Connie so that they could work together on solving the problem.

For any child, healthy relationships with teachers and other adults are key to the development of a positive self-image. When children move, such nurturing relationships may be lost. One of the ways you can ease your children's transition to a new school and community, then, is to help them develop good relationships with new adult role models—teachers, coaches, band directors, Sunday school teachers, neighbors, and any other adults with whom your children will have contact.

Once they have helped your kids, don't forget to thank these people for their effort. My husband and I still keep in touch with several teachers and other adults who have enriched our children's lives in our former communities. More than once, an adult who has taken one of our children under his wing after a move has become a lasting family friend.

Make the most of your temporary home.

Nothing is worth more than this day.
—Johann Wolfgang von Goethe

How many times as a child did you impatiently anticipate those splendid events like Christmas and birthdays, only to be brought back to reality by your parents' admonition: "Don't wish your life away." I have repeated my parents' words to my own children many times, as they express the wish that the next special occasion were here *right now!* The older I get, the more I realize how critical it is that we make the most of the *process* of life, that we enjoy the preparation for each event as much as the event itself, and that we appreciate everyday occurrences as much as special occasions. Although I don't think my children will fully appreciate the importance of this until they are adults, we talk frequently about how crucial it is to enjoy the path as much as the destination—for example, how it is as much fun to make the cookie dough as it is to eat the cookies, or how putting together the jigsaw puzzle is as enjoyable as mounting the end product on the wall.

Enjoying the moment is particularly challenging when you're

preparing to move. Too often, you feel as if your life is on hold—
as if you are in limbo. Before you move, you can sleep and eat in
your house, but you can't really *live* in it, because the real-estate
agent may want to show it to a prospective buyer at a moment's
notice. You don't want to start any new projects, because you know
you won't be able to finish them before you move. You may avoid
spending time with your friends, because being around them
reminds you that you will soon be saying goodbye. And you may be
feeling too gloomy to have fun with other people, anyway.
Children, even young ones, have feelings like this, too. They get
tired of having to keep their toys put away, and of having their nap-
times and mealtimes changed to accommodate visits from prospective house buyers.

When your move involves a stay in temporary housing before
you can move into your permanent residence, enjoying the
moment becomes even more challenging. Leaving your old home
has likely left you feeling unsettled, and all you want to do now is
move into your new home so you can begin to plant some roots.
For many families, this isn't possible right away. Our family has
stayed in a variety of lodgings while we were waiting for a new
house to be available; we've spent several days in a motel, several
weeks in an extended-stay hotel, and five months in an apartment.
We've also spent time visiting Randy in hotels and apartments
when he's moved before the rest of us. There's nothing about a
hotel or a furnished apartment that seems personal. Your child
may not mind at first, but she will get frustrated when she doesn't
have the toy she wants to play with, the pants she wants to wear, or
the recording she wants to watch or hear. If the temporary home
is with relatives or friends, having to follow someone else's rules
may quickly become stressful for her.

When you find yourself staring at the hotel or apartment walls,
wishing away the transition period before you move into your new
home, it's time to take a deep breath and start reframing your perspective. Remind yourself that you and your kids have everything
you need to be happy right now—not once you move out of the
cramped apartment and into a new house full of familiar belong-

ings, not once you have established a strong support system of new friends, but *now*. Even if you'll be living in a temporary residence for only a few weeks or months, make it feel like home.

Likely, you'll know before you move that you'll be in temporary housing, so pack a couple of boxes filled with some of your favorite family treasures. Place framed pictures of your children around the rooms. Bring your own comforters and pillows so your sleeping areas look familiar. Put some flowers in a vase on the kitchen table. Stick some of the kids' drawings on the wall with removable tape or putty, or on the refrigerator with magnets. And make sure your children's favorite books and toys are readily available.

When Laurie and her family arrive at a temporary house, one of the first things she unpacks and displays is a refrigerator magnet that says, "Home is where the Air Force sends you." This is a constant reminder to both Laurie and her children that, regardless of the setting, they are at home as long as their family is together.

We often find that living in temporary housing feels almost like a vacation to the kids. I spend less time on chores, such as clean-

---

WAYS TO MAKE THE MOST OF YOUR TEMPORARY HOME

Place framed family pictures around the rooms.

Bring your own comforters and pillows so sleeping areas look familiar.

Put a basket of fruit or a vase of flowers on the kitchen table.

Use your favorite refrigerator magnets to display your children's artwork.

Clean less, and play more.

Relax some family rules—eat pizza for breakfast, or have a family slumber party in the living room.

ing and cooking, so I can spend more time with the kids. Unless you're staying with friends or relatives, allow yourself to let go of the need to have the rooms clean and tidy. My kids still remember with joy the time we were visiting Randy in his temporary apartment in Fort Lauderdale before we made the move from Louisville. Randy ran out of dishwasher detergent and so decided to use regular liquid dish soap instead. Soon the entire kitchen was filled knee-high with bubbles. Just as I started to grab a mop, I noticed the magical look on my children's faces. So we forgot about cleaning and played. The kitchen was a child's paradise of bubbles. We cleaned up eventually, but only after enjoying an afternoon of play.

> **"Getting things on the walls makes a big difference. As soon as you hang some pictures and put a basket of fresh fruit on the table, you feel more settled. Then it's easier to relax and help the kids feel more at home."**
>
> CONNIE, SINGLE
> MOTHER OF FOUR BOYS

Maximize your sense of adventure while living in temporary housing. Take advantage of being out of your routine; do things you normally wouldn't do. Make peanut-butter-and-jelly sandwiches for a picnic dinner outdoors on a blanket. Take the sheets and blankets off the beds, and have the whole family sleep one night in the living room. Let the kids eat leftover pizza for breakfast. Take advantage of special features of your temporary home, such as a swimming pool or hot tub. If the premises aren't pleasant or neighbors are sensitive to noise, get out and explore the area—parks, museums, shops, and so on—before the family gets busy with lessons and social commitments.

One of Mark's most enjoyable birthday parties was when we were living in a small apartment in Baltimore, waiting for our house to be built. I debated even letting him have a party, because we had been in Baltimore only a couple of months and he hadn't made many friends. Besides, I thought, the apartment was much too small for a five-year-old's birthday party. When Mark insisted that he wanted a party, I suggested holding it at a nearby McDonald's. He wanted it at our apartment. Realizing that a party could be a good way to help his transition, Randy and I relented. Although I am a planner by nature, I couldn't think of any games for a cramped apartment and lacked energy for organizing a party. So we decided to simply serve pizza. The two hours flew by as Mark and his six new friends and his sisters ate at our very crowded table and then played volleyball with a balloon over the living-room couch. They would occasionally stop to run an obstacle course (that included crawling into our new puppy's crate) before resuming their balloon volleyball game. Mark's party was a hit. In this era of overscheduling kids' activities, I realized, children really appreciate the opportunity to make their own fun.

Thinking of the five months we spent in that cramped apartment brings back happy memories: Mark's party. Training our new puppy. Coming back from taking the girls to school and finding Mark and my grandparents, who were visiting from Florida, hiding in a tent made out of blankets and chairs in the middle of the living room. Using cookie trays to sled down a slight incline outside after the first snow. Making friends with the elderly gentleman who lived next door. In fact, we had so much fun in that apartment that, two weeks after we moved into our new house, Sarah and Mark asked whether we could move back to the apartment!

Living in temporary housing can be a great opportunity to do things you normally wouldn't do. Look for the fun and adventure in each moment. Help your children appreciate that, in the words of Goethe, "nothing is worth more than this day." Make the most of it—whether you're in temporary housing or in your new home.

15

Don't wait for new friends to come to you.

The only way to have a friend is to be one.
—Ralph Waldo Emerson, *Essays*

Ten-year-old Geordan believes in taking the direct approach when he is making friends following a move. He just walks up to a new person and says, "Hi, I'm Geordan. I just moved to the neighborhood, and I don't have friends. Will you be my friend?"

Not all of us are comfortable being so forthcoming. As a naturally shy person myself, I feel awkward when initiating new relationships. And, unfortunately, I am probably the most outgoing member of my immediate family. The three kids and Randy—even more so than me—are naturally quiet and reserved until they feel acclimated to a new situation.

When we started moving frequently, however, I realized very quickly that—pardon my grammar—shy ain't gonna cut it! Sitting at home and waiting for friends to come to you doesn't usually work. Moving to Louisville spoiled me in this regard, because people in Louisville are experts in Southern hospitality. Within a few days of moving there, our doorbell was ringing regularly with neighbors who introduced themselves, welcomed us to the neighborhood, and, usually, presented us with a plate of homemade cookies. Expecting similar treatment when we moved into our new home in Coral Springs, a suburb of Fort Lauderdale, we waited for the doorbell to ring. And waited. And waited. No one came. No cookies. No welcome. Not even a friendly wave. After a couple of weeks, I faced the painful realization that neighbors wouldn't be showing up on my doorstep to warmly welcome us to the community.

So I decided to overcome my inhibitions and start initiating conversations myself. When I caught a glimpse of a girl who looked about Sarah's age going into the house across the street, I immediately grabbed my kids, crossed the street, rang the door-

 WAYS CHILDREN CAN FIND NEW FRIENDS

Walk or ride through the neighborhood and introduce yourself to other kids.

Set up a lemonade stand or hold a toy sale in your driveway.

Invite other kids to play on your swing set or shoot baskets with you.

Host a get-acquainted party at your house.

Spend time at the neighborhood park or community pool.

Join an organized group, such as Scouts or 4-H.

Sign up for a sports team, or join the school band.

Get involved in school clubs, such as drama, chess, or debate.

Bring extra treats in your school lunch, and offer them to people at your table.

Participate in youth and family activities at a nearby church, temple, or mosque.

bell, and introduced us. I then invited the girl to come over with her mother to play on our new swing set, which they were happy to do. Likewise, I began initiating conversations with moms at the playground, fast-food restaurants, and the children's section of the local library.

One of the most important things kids can do when they're try-ing to make friends is to make themselves available. Encourage your children to go out-side and be visible—to ride bikes or skate up and down the street or play with the dog in the front yard. Let the kids have a lemonade stand or a toy sale to draw other children to your yard. Get some outdoor equipment that encourages cooperative play, such as a swing set, soccer net, wading pool, sandbox, or bas-ketball hoop. Walk through the neighbor-hood and look for signs of other kids. Spend a lot of time at the neighborhood park or the community pool. If your child isn't comfort-able initiating conversations with other kids himself, do it for him. The more he sees you do this, the easier it will become for him.

> "My mom and dad encourage me to get involved in numerous activities in our new town to make getting to know people a whole lot easier. Right off the bat, they start their search for churches with good youth pro-grams, competitive sports teams, advanced music programs, and other community groups that alleviate the stress of trying to make new friends."
>
> REBECCA, AGE 14

Children love parties, so host a get-acquainted party at your house. Help your child make invitations, and then deliver them door to door in your neighborhood. If it's summertime, have an ice-cream sundae party in the driveway. If it's winter and snow-ing, host a sledding party, with hot chocolate and cookies after-ward. With a little effort, you can pull off a fun event that will encourage other children to get to know your child. Your party might be so much fun that you'll decide to make it an annual event.

Children often have an easier time doing things together rather than just talking, so help your kids get involved with groups of children who share their interests. There are innumerable organ-izations in which your kids might get involved: sports, scouting,

4-H, religious youth groups, library story times, Mommy and Me, Young Life, homeschool co-ops, community theater, and many more. Talk to the group leaders before your child attends for the first time, and enlist their help in making sure your child feels welcome. Your children will likely find friends easily through these activities.

One of the things I stress to my kids when they're trying to make new friends is that they shouldn't limit themselves to children who have best-friend potential. Even if your kids have little in common with children they meet, they can still hang out with these kids until they find friends who share more of their interests. To some people this may seem exploitive, but I tell my children that as long as they remain polite and friendly with their old friends once they have made new ones, it's perfectly okay to keep looking for people with whom they have more in common. Besides, you can learn valuable things from people who are different from you, and often it's the person with whom you didn't really hit it off on your first encounter who ends up becoming your close friend.

> **"When you're making friends, don't be shy. Just go up to somebody and say, 'Hi, my name's _____. What's yours?'"**
>
> MARK, AGE 10

As you are seeking out new relationships for your kids, don't just look for the obvious ones. Neighbors without children or with grown children can become great friends for the whole family. They might enjoy cooking or doing crafts with the kids, or they may pay generously for pet-sitting or lawn-mowing. One of my newly married friends moved into a new community and was excited when the next-door neighbor came and introduced herself. The neighbor's first question was "Do you have children?" When my friend said no, the neighbor said, "Oh," and turned around and walked away. Besides being very rude, this neighbor lost a chance to have her children get to know a really neat person!

Once you've surrounded your child with opportunities to be around other children, it's time for them to begin making friends. Remember, as your children learn the skills of making friends, you are their best role model. Practice the following skills, discuss them with your children, and offer ample encouragement as they begin to practice them themselves:

- Smile warmly and maintain eye contact.

- Be positive and upbeat. Don't whine about how much better things were where you used to live.

- Practice good listening skills. Ask questions that show you are interested in what the other person is saying.

- Look for commonalities. I haven't found a person yet with whom I couldn't find at least one thing that we shared. Do they like the same music? Do they have pets? What do they like to do for fun? What places have they visited? What foods do they like?

- Be yourself. Don't pretend to be someone you aren't just to make a friend.

- Act confident, even if you're not. This may seem to contradict the advice to be yourself, but often the best way to start feeling confident is to start acting confident.

- Learn the art of conversation. Initiating a conversation is the first step; keeping a conversation going may take some practice. Ask open-ended questions. Elaborate when someone asks you a question, and then end with a question for her. For example, if someone asks whether you had a nice summer, don't just say, "Yeah." Say, "Yes, we stayed at a cool cabin by a lake, and I got to water-ski for the first time. What did you do?"

- Respect people's boundaries. Don't bring up topics that are too personal, such as what grade they got on the last test, which boy they have a crush on, or what kind of house they live in. And don't continue to try to talk to someone who is obviously not interested.

The more your children begin practicing these skills, the easier it will become. Trust me—I've had to step outside my comfort zone to practice these skills myself!

16

Even if you know this is a short-term move, approach it as if it's not.

Wherever you go, go with all your heart.
—Confucius

When I tell people how many times we have moved, one of the first questions they often ask is "Are you going to be here long?" I sometimes get the impression that people are trying to decide whether or not a friendship with my family is worth the investment. They don't want to get attached only to have the friendship end when we move away. I usually respond, honestly, "We hope to stay here for a long time."

Although my husband and I were aware on some level that he was climbing the corporate ladder, we didn't consciously go into each move anticipating that his next promotion would involve another move. In fact, we were in a state of denial about it—or at least I was. I remember driving past a street in Atlanta named Dunmovin and afterward telling my neighbors that my family should have moved to that street, because we were definitely "dun movin'!" And I still have the Christmas letter I wrote our first year in Baltimore in which I told our friends to throw their Wite-Out away because our address wasn't going to change again! I truly anticipated that each move would be our last.

Maybe this was my coping mechanism. Maybe if we had been told, "You will live in Fort Lauderdale for 16 months, then move to Atlanta for 16 months, then move to Topeka for 16 months," we wouldn't have become as ingrained as we did in each community. But I'm glad that wasn't the case. When I think of the lifelong friends we've made in each of our short-term communities—and of the people with whom we no longer keep in touch but who had a significant impact on our lives—I know without a doubt that the pain of having to say goodbye was worth the friendships that we developed.

Several years ago I attempted to befriend the mother of a girl who joined Becca's class in the middle of the school year. I could tell that "Judy" was intelligent and kindhearted by the comments she made at school meetings, but she seemed lonely. Every time I invited her to participate in an activity with my friends, however, she would politely decline, saying she had other plans. One day as we were talking at the school, I mentioned that I was thinking about writing a book about moving, and asked whether she might have any ideas for it. Judy's husband, like mine, was in a fast-track career that had involved several moves in a short period of time, and he and Judy had been told that they would be in their current community for only 12 to 18 months. Judy's advice was this: "Don't get too attached, because then it hurts too much to have to leave." I never became anything more to Judy than a casual acquaintance, and we politely said our goodbyes when her husband was transferred the following year. But it strikes me as sad that someone would rather spend a year of her life being lonely and isolated than risk feeling hurt when saying goodbye. And it strikes me as even sadder that Judy encouraged her children to stay similarly detached. I guess she felt it would be easier for all of them to say goodbye to a miserable year than a fulfilling one.

Although she disagrees with it now, Mary, a military mom, understands how Judy reached the decision that she did. Mary's family lived near Washington, D.C., for 11 months when her daughter,

Emily, was seven. Because they had long-time family friends close enough to spend time with on the weekends, and because Mary knew her family would be there such a short time, she decided not to encourage Emily to make friends at school. Mary's rationale was that the next move would be easier if Emily didn't make any attachments. With a house so small that, as Mary describes it, she could vacuum the entire house with the cord plugged into one electrical outlet, she told Emily that they didn't have enough room for her to invite any school friends over. Emily followed her Mom's lead so well that the school counselor called to express concern about Emily's lack of attachment to other children. If she could turn back the clock, Mary says, she would handle the situation differently; she would encourage Emily to make new friends. "Besides," Mary acknowledges, "it didn't work anyway. By the end of the year, Emily had made friends and had to painfully tell them goodbye."

> "We lived in Topeka for only 16 months, but that is where I met my best friend, Alex. If I hadn't been willing to make friends while we were there, I would have missed out."
>
> SARAH, AGE 13

Interestingly, Rebecca, Sarah, and Mark tell me that, of all the times they have told new friends about their moving history, only once did another child ask about any future moving plans. To kids, as a general rule, life is what is happening right now. Tomorrow doesn't matter when you're playing a football game, skateboarding through the neighborhood, or playing with your Barbie dolls. Becca has known from the day they met that her best friend, Katie, would have to move from Tampa in three years, but that fact was irrelevant as their friendship developed. When the end of the three years drew near, Becca began planning a memorable surprise goodbye party. She delighted in watching Katie's face light up as all of her friends gathered to say goodbye. Becca also spent hours creating a memory book celebrating their friendship to send with Katie when she moved. Five months after Katie moved, she came back to spend Thanksgiving week with our family.

Alfred, Lord Tennyson's words may seem clichéd, but truly "'tis better to have loved and lost than never to have loved at all."

Anyone embroiled in a bitter divorce would likely question the legitimacy of this philosophy, but most divorced people end up remarrying eventually. So even people who have been badly burned through divorce decide it's worth the risk to love again. And the pain involved in leaving friends when moving doesn't generally rival that of a divorce.

It does hurt to say goodbye. A couple of friends have gotten angry with me when I told them my family was moving. And I mean really angry, to the point that they wouldn't talk to me for several days. They felt I had betrayed them by telling them I thought we would be living in their city for a long time. But eventually they realized their anger was really misdirected sadness and a feeling of loss. Several moves later, we still maintain our friendship.

Life is unpredictable; none of us really knows what is going to happen tomorrow. Do you want to teach your children through example to spend their lives living in fear that tomorrow may bring pain or sadness? Or do you want to show your children how to make the most of every precious moment of life? The ancient advice of Confucius stands true today: "Wherever you go, go with all your heart." Whether you will stay in your new home for six months, six years, or six decades, open yourself up to all the opportunities for happiness your community has to offer. And encourage your children to do the same.

17

Create a sense of belonging in your new home.

I am a part of all that I have met.
—Alfred, Lord Tennyson, "Ulysses"

One of the most frequent complaints I hear from people who have had bad experiences in moving is that they didn't fit in because the locals never accepted them. People in some regions, undoubtedly, embrace newcomers more readily than people in others, but wherever you move you can do things to give yourself and your children a sense of belonging. As in the old adage "When in Rome, do as the Romans," sometimes you have to act as though you fit in before you begin to feel, and people begin to treat you, as though you really belong.

Moving to another country probably presents the most difficult challenges in attaining a sense of belonging. A different language and culture can make your family feel painfully isolated. No one I know has done a better job of acclimating to her new culture than my friend Debby Wadas, who moved to Germany with her husband and three children at the same time that my family moved to Tampa. At first intending to return to the United States after a three-year military stint, the family decided to sign on for another three-year term so they could remain in Germany longer.

Debby had the advantage of having learned German from her German-speaking parents. But she set the stage for developing her family's sense of belonging by greeting her German neighbors and inviting them over for coffee and cake. She found that walking, biking, and joining hiking clubs were great ways to start conversations and eventually win their neighbors' acceptance. She respected local customs related to conversational boundaries; she never initiated talk of politics or religion, and she talked of what she liked about Germany even when she was missing something about the United States. Although Debby and her husband decided to enroll their two older children in an American school to ease their adjustment, they studied and practiced German, and Debby's youngest child attended a German kindergarten, where she was fully immersed in the language and culture. Debby's family also demonstrated respect for local values, including neatness and cleanliness. The family's extra-good care of their house and yard included a lot of sweeping (nowhere outside of German villages have I seen so many people sweeping!). Debby's husband labored so much to keep their yard looking tidy that the neighbors fondly nicknamed him *Fleissig*, "Hard-working." The respect and care that Debby's family showed to their neighbors was soon returned, and today some of the family's dearest friends are people they have met since moving to Germany.

Debby has helped her children fully appreciate not just Germany but all of Europe. Every few months I receive an e-mail message about the family's most recent trip across the Continent, with an organized tour group or on their own. In the three years they have lived in Germany, Debby's family has visited Scotland, England, France, Italy, Spain, Denmark, Holland, Luxembourg, Poland, and Belgium. Soon they will visit Salzburg, Austria, to see where *The Sound of Music* was filmed. How enriched the lives of Debby's children have been through their move overseas! German culture and the European experience will be an important part of their identity when they return to the United States.

Mary, another military mom, feels that a willingness to share American culture as well as respect for the local culture enabled her family to experience a sense of belonging overseas. One of her favorite memories is of their first Halloween in Italy: Mary delighted her Italian neighbors by dressing her children in spooky costumes and walking them door to door. Like Debby, Mary and her family respected local customs. In Italy, for example, businesses close for most of the afternoon so people can go home and take a rest. Mary learned very quickly not to let her children play outside during this time, so as not to disturb their neighbors. She also ensured that her family members dressed according to the local customs, which included never wearing shorts in public. These small demonstrations of respect for the local culture can go a long way in helping a family gain acceptance in a community.

> **"When you move to an overseas country, try to learn the language of that country, because then it is easier to make friends!"**
>
> NATALIE, AGE 6

Whether you move overseas or within the United States, you and your family can deepen your sense of belonging by learning about local history and geography. Visit museums and the capital city, study maps, wander back roads and graveyards, peruse books of old photos in the regional history section of the public library, and check out a book of stories about local personalities from the past. Visit historical sites where volunteers or staff dress in historical costumes and demonstrate traditional crafts. After a move within the United States, learn your new state's motto and nickname (the Hoosier State, the Sunshine State, the Sunflower State), and learn to identify the state bird, tree, flower, and flag. If your third- or fourth-grade child is studying state and local history in school, encourage him to be a teaching resource for other family members. As your children become familiar with local history, they may find that they know as much or more about the community as people who have lived there all their lives.

Attending local festivals is another great way to learn about local customs and to begin to feel that you're a part of the community. One of the most enthralling local events my family has experienced is Derby Week in Louisville, Kentucky. The whole downtown shuts down for the week of celebrations that culminates in the first of the Triple Crown races. First comes the Fireworks Festival (the largest fireworks display in the country—or at least it was when we lived in Louisville), then the Derby Parade, and then the pre-Derby Kentucky Oaks Day at the Races. When we left Louisville, we missed the excitement of Derby Week so much that we have since hosted Derby parties at each place we've lived. The people we've invited have usually asked, "What's a Derby party?" (At a Derby party, you watch a two-minute horse race together and then socialize for the rest of the evening.) But they have enjoyed the celebration so much that, in more than one city, our friends have hosted a Derby party without us when we moved away! In this small way, we have shared our pride in Louisville with friends around the country. Visit the local Chamber of Commerce or tourist office for a calendar of events like Derby Week.

 WAYS TO CREATE A SENSE OF BELONGING IN YOUR NEW HOME

Learn about local history and traditions.

Read the local newspaper.

Attend festivals and other kid-friendly events.

Explore nearby historical sites and tourist attractions.

Enjoy the local cuisine.

Cheer on the professional, college, and high-school sports teams.

Frequent local restaurants and businesses, and get to know the owners.

If you move to another country, learn the language and respect the customs.

Take part in small events as well as big ones. Attend community Easter egg hunts, school carnivals and plays, holiday picnics, and children's parades. Attend the county fair, and encourage your child to enter his homemade cookies or homegrown carrots. If your children are old enough, help with a beach cleanup or an Arbor Day tree planting. Most churches host child- and family-friendly events that are open to the general public—bazaars, Christmas plays, and the like. Subscribe to the local paper so you'll know what's happening in your community. If your family particularly enjoys an event, consider volunteering with the organization that sponsors it.

One of the most enjoyable (and sometimes fattening) ways to develop a sense of belonging in a new community is by learning about local foods. When Laurie's family lived in Germany, they looked forward to their German friends' raclette parties, in which families socialize while potatoes slowly cook with cheese, vegetables, and meat. Many American cities host fundraising events, such as our Taste of Tampa, in which participants get to sample foods from local restaurants; take the kids, and encourage them to try foods they've never tasted before. When your family wants dinner out, pass up the urge to pull into the parking lot of a chain restaurant, and go for a mom-and-pop restaurant instead (Sarah's favorite restaurant near Atlanta was actually called Moms and Pops!). If you become regulars at one of these restaurants, you'll get to know the owners and long-time employees, who can be great resources for information about your community. Take your family to a community breakfast, spaghetti dinner, or bean supper. Try the produce at farm stands and U-pick orchards and fields. Feast on blue crabs in Maryland, cheesesteaks in Philadelphia, seafood in Florida, or corn on the cob in the Midwest.

Another great way to develop a sense of pride and belonging in a new community is by following the local sports teams—professional, college, or high school. Attend games in the sport your family enjoys, and cheer for the local team. Buy your kids T-shirts and caps featuring your city's favorite teams. Team loyalty can be a touchy subject among family members who have moved, because kids often keep a link to a past community through allegiance to its teams. If this is the case for your kids, don't ask them to switch loyalties, but encourage them to consider having two favorite teams in the league, or a new favorite team in a new sport, or a new favorite in a new league (such as high school rather than college). By all means, discourage your children from flaunting any victories of their old home team over the local team. Because of the bad blood created when the owner of the Baltimore Colts moved the football team to Indianapolis in the middle of the night, in Baltimore we avoided mentioning that we were Indianapolis Colts fans until we were very secure in our friendships! And we were cheering right along with our neighbors when the Baltimore Ravens won the Super Bowl in 2001.

Every community has unique qualities in which residents take some pride. By taking advantage of all the special things your new community has to offer, you will help your children develop the sense that they truly belong.

18

Always remember what's most important.

M is for I love momy!
—Mark, age 7

R andy and I refer to it as the dreaded phone call. You're busy doing parent things—giving the kids a bath, helping them with their homework, picking them up from baseball practice. Life, in general, is good. And then the phone rings. You answer it cheerfully, thinking it's a neighbor or one of your kids' friends. You wouldn't even mind if it turned out to be a telemarketer. You say hello, and there is no answer at first, and then your spouse speaks those terrible words: "We need to talk." If you've moved only once or twice, this story may be unfamiliar, but if your career or your spouse's has made your family nomadic, I'm sure you get the gist. When Randy utters those four simple words, my life turns upside down. I know immediately that I am being asked to consider a move. This means that everything else over the next few hours, or probably the next few days, will have to wait as we painstakingly struggle with a decision whether or not to move. This also means that, if our decision is yes (which it usually is), our lives will change, once again, forever.

I remember the scene exactly when I got the dreaded phone call in Baltimore. Randy was out of town on business. Sarah and Becca had just finished their homework and were on their way to the basement to play. Mark was sitting at the kitchen table practicing his writing, and I was loading the dinner dishes into the dishwasher. The phone rang, and I answered it, oblivious to any possibility that the call could be life-altering. When I heard Randy utter *the* words, I told Mark to go play with his sisters, and I took the portable phone into the bedroom, where I could take in the news in private. About 30 minutes into our call, when my face was stained with tears and my stomach filled with knots, Mark sneaked into my room, tugged at my shirt sleeve, and whispered, "Mom." I looked at him long enough to see there was no blood or broken bones, told him the call was very important, and said that I would come out to talk with him in a little bit.

After 30 more minutes of trying to absorb the shock of the situation, Randy and I decided to talk more after the kids went to bed. I wiped my tears, washed my face with cold water, and went out to find Mark. There he was, sitting patiently at the kitchen table, with a sheepish grin on his seven-year-old face. He handed me a card that he had made for me. On the front was a happy face and a picture of a very round me (I knew it was me because there were four arrows that said, "Momy, Momy, Momy, Momy"). Inside the card he had written—

I love you so much Momy!
this card is for you I hope you like it.
*   M is for I love momy!*
*   O is for oh I like momy's smile!*
*   M is for momy treats me good.*
I love, love, love, love, love, love, love, love, you. I hope you love
me that much to. From Mark. to Momy.

How could he have possibly known how desperately I needed a reminder about what is important in life? I could have moved to Timbuktu at that moment and been happy, as long as my family was with me. My barely-seven-year-old son's timing was perfect, and he gave me a priceless gift to help keep my priorities in line. Four years later, I still keep that card next to my desk where I can see it every day.

Being part of a family who loves you is what's most important. Each time we move, *family* becomes our mantra. Yes, friends are important. But while we each make a multitude of friends in our lifetime, we have only one family. It is the responsibility of family members to care for one another. It often happens that, soon after we move, a friend whom one of our children was most reluctant to leave behind ends up moving away with his or her family. When this happens, I point out to the kids that friends may come and go, but our family will always be there for them.

> "One of the pep talks I give my children each time we move is: 'The most important people you'll ever know are living right in this house with you. You won't share the same memories with anyone else in your lifetime.'"
>
> LISA, MOTHER OF THREE

During a recent soccer tournament, one of the other moms rode in the car with our family to a soccer field about 30 minutes away. My kids were joking around with each other and playing games, as they normally do. When we arrived at the field, the other mom said to me, "I've never been around siblings who have so much fun together." Her comment caught me off-guard, because my kids argue and irritate one another as much as any brothers and sisters do. As I thought about her words, though, I realized that Rebecca, Sarah, and Mark share a special bond, as do many siblings whose families have moved a lot. My kids have spent many months after moves being one another's only friends. They have learned to rely on one another when they didn't have any other children on whom to depend. Moving has brought our family closer together.

For 19 years, Connie and her husband raised their four sons together. When their marriage suddenly dissolved, Connie was faced with the challenge of re-creating the family unit as a single mom. Connie knew that she must first reassure her sons that their father would always be an important part of their lives, even though they were now living six hours away from him. But she also had to lead the family in regrouping, by directly addressing the changes they would have to deal with in a single-parent home. During a family meeting shortly after they moved to Nashville, Connie explained to her boys that, because she was now working full time, she needed their full cooperation with family chores and responsibilities; she would depend on the older boys, for example, to watch the younger ones and to help them with homework. She acknowledged that finances would be tight and that they would have to cut some expenditures, such as for meals out, games, and new clothes. Connie emphasized, however, that this temporary struggle did not change the basic foundation of their family. In fact, their family unit would now have to be even stronger to face this challenge. The thing to always remember, Connie told her sons, is that, regardless of the circumstances, they *were* going to make it as a family.

> "I called a family meeting shortly after we moved and offered encouragement to my boys that, even though they're physically apart, they are still loved by their dad and grandparents. I acknowledged that we would have to make some changes, but that we were going to make it as a family."
>
> CONNIE, SINGLE MOTHER OF FOUR BOYS

Moving can help your children understand that the love of a family is never ending. It can also help them see that, even beyond the family, love pervades. I have come to realize that love, beauty, and contentment can be constant in our lives, even though the forms in which we experience them may change. As we have moved from state to state, and mourned the loss of everyday relationships with beautiful people we have had to leave behind, our faith that we would find love, beauty, and contentment in our new home has always been fulfilled. This love has taken a variety of shapes and forms, many of them unexpected.

When your children reach a low point during the transition to a new home, remind them that they have a family who loves them no matter what, and that now they have a chance to meet new friends who will love them, too. Love is truly what makes a house a home, regardless of where it is.

19

If the resources you need aren't there, take a leadership role in creating them.

Nothing will ever be attempted,
if all possible objections must first be overcome.

—Samuel Johnson,
The History of Rasselas, Prince of Abissinia

Some organized children's activities—dance classes, martial arts, library story times, recreational sports, and scouting—are standard in American communities. Still, you may find that resources on which your family relied in your prior community are lacking in the new one. Having to give up favorite activities may make your children resent the move more than they would otherwise. With a little initiative, however, you may be able to create the resources your kids need in your new community.

Maybe the homeschool group in your last community sponsored monthly social events for the kids, and your new homeschool group provides only classes. Find out whether the members might support organized social activities—such as a Valentine's Day dance, a Halloween party, park or beach days—and then offer to organize the activities for a few months. Even if only a few families attend initially, your kids may meet the new friends they have been looking for.

Or maybe your children looked forward to participating in a neighborhood Independence Day bicycle parade in your last town, but there is nothing of its kind in your new community. Again, consider organizing the event yourself.

When my family moved to the Tampa area, we found that girls' basketball wasn't nearly as big as it had been in Baltimore. Not happy with any of the local resources, Randy decided to form an all-girl basketball team to compete in the YMCA recreational league. Until then, the few interested girls were intermingled with the boys, who too often were uninterested in passing the ball to anyone of the female persuasion. For the new team, Randy recruited girls mainly from Sarah's soccer team. They had a great season, although it was a little embarrassing when the Y had to bring in special referees because—according to the boys' parents—the girls played too rough.

When Laurie's family moved to Germany, she noticed that the military families and the German families in her neighborhood didn't interact much. Realizing that both groups were missing out on a great opportunity for making new friends, she and her husband, Bruce, convinced one of the German families to help them organize a neighborhood block party. Although they had never heard of the concept, the German family soon caught Bruce and Laurie's enthusiasm for the idea; the German husband, a musician, even got his band to play at the event. Bruce and Laurie invited their military friends, the German family invited their German friends, and everyone was amazed at what a great time they had. This event was the beginning of many intercultural friendships among the children and the adults. A year later, the whole neighborhood helped with preparations for the second annual block party. Even after Bruce and Laurie's family moved back to the United States, the neighborhood continued the block-party tradition.

When Randy and I moved our family from Fort Lauderdale to Atlanta, we left behind an adult friend who had lived with us part time and who had watched Mark while I volunteered at Becca and Sarah's school once a week. In Atlanta, the girls still wanted me to help in their classes, but I had no one to care for Mark. I called every family child-care provider and daycare center that I could find, but none of them was willing to take Mark for only a few hours a week. Besides, I hated the thought of paying someone to watch one of my children so I could volunteer at the school of another.

I began to think creatively. We had moved to a neighborhood with hundreds of houses and, from what I had observed, many stay-at-home moms with young children. From the number of For Sale signs in the yards, I assumed there were a lot of corporate families coming and going. Other mothers in the neighborhood, I realized, might share my problem and frustration. So I talked with a few of the moms at the park and, with their endorsement, decided to organize a neighborhood child-care co-op. I put an article in our neighborhood newsletter announcing a meeting to be held at the nearby McDonald's (with a children's play area). About 10 moms came to the first meeting. By the end of the second meeting, we had agreed upon policies and officially launched the neighborhood babysitting co-op.

> "Our first year in Germany, we noticed that the German families and the military families in our neighborhood didn't really interact that much. So we organized a block party to help everyone get to know their neighbors."
>
> LAURIE, MOTHER OF TWO

For the first six months, I led the co-op by distributing a list of parents' names, phone numbers, and children's ages and keeping track of members' usage hours. I also helped organize weekly get-togethers at McDonald's, which allowed members to review the records for accuracy and newcomers to get to know the other parents before joining the co-op. There were many kinks to work out in the system, but establishing the co-op allowed me to volunteer at Becca and Sarah's school without having to pay for child care, while Mark enjoyed playing in a neighbor's home with children his age for a few hours a week.

After six months, I turned over leadership responsibility to another co-op member, because by that time I had found friends with whom I could share child care less formally. Although I heard that the co-op began to fizzle about the time we were moving away, I hope that another action-oriented parent came along to revive this great resource for newcomers to the neighborhood.

As you're assessing your family's needs, don't forget about your own. One resource I have developed in several communities is a women's bunco group. Bunco is a mindless dice game that serves as a great excuse for women to get together once a month and socialize. I was introduced to bunco in Louisville, where I soon eagerly looked forward to each monthly women's night out. When I discovered that bunco groups were lacking in our subsequent communities, I started my own neighborhood groups. They have been great hits! In fact, seven years after I left Topeka and four years after I left Baltimore, both bunco groups are going strong. When I left Baltimore, the bunco group gave me a "bunco starter kit" so I would have the necessary supplies to begin a new group when we moved.

There are several benefits to taking a leadership role in creating resources you need in a new community. First of all, the resources you create will help meet your own family's needs. Second, these resources will help meet the needs of other families as well. Finally, you are demonstrating for your children the importance of being a doer. Rather than sitting around and complaining that what you need isn't there, you are taking the responsibility for meeting your own needs by enlisting the help of people around you. Someday your children will follow your example.

20

Send out your own welcome wagon.

Make new friends, but keep the old;
one is silver and the other gold.
—Traditional lyric

After months of planning and rehearsing, the day of the big dance recital finally arrived. When we had moved to Fort Lauderdale, Becca decided to continue the dance lessons she had begun in Louisville, and Sarah decided to join her big sister at dance classes. We found a reputable dance studio, and we enrolled Becca in the kindergarten-age class and Sarah in the four-year-old class. As we prepared for the first recital, we learned what a big ordeal these recitals could be. The three-hour-long event, held at a large auditorium, was complete with expensive costumes, video-tapes for purchase, and a lot of proud relatives in attendance. At Sarah's final dress rehearsal, the instructor explained that she wanted the girls to wear pajamas for the second dance, a lullaby. When asked whether the girls should all wear the same type of pajamas, the instructor said that, for an appealing variety, each girl could wear her own favorite pajamas.

Sarah was excited about getting to wear her powder blue, long-sleeved Sleeping Beauty pajamas for the second dance. Randy and I each breathed a sigh of relief after the first performance, in which Sarah actually kept to the beat and remembered almost all of the steps. When the curtains rose for the second number, our mouths dropped in horror: There were nine girls in cute, matching spaghetti-strap baby-doll pajamas and Sarah in her suddenly not quite-so-cute floor-length Sleeping Beauty pajamas. Her mismatched outfit wasn't nearly as painful to look at, though, as the humiliated look on her face. Apparently, all the moms had gotten together after the dress rehearsal and decided that the performance would look cuter if the girls wore matching pajamas. All the moms, that is, except me. Together, they had decided to buy matching pajamas for their daughters.

Did the other mothers intentionally leave me out of the loop so that my daughter would be humiliated at the dance recital? Surely not. Were the other moms so absorbed in their own clique that they forgot they were leaving one member of the dance team out of their planning efforts? Absolutely.

I hope that you won't be involved in a situation that so blatantly casts your child as an outsider. If you have moved before, though, you know what it feels like to be apart from the group initially. For your children, there are the first few lunches in the school cafeteria, where they don't have friends with whom to sit. Or, if your child is fortunate enough to have an assigned seat, she must awkwardly pretend that she is part of the conversation even though none of the comments are directed to her. There are the recesses in which the kickball teams and the jump-rope partners have already been chosen, and your child has to act like he's happy playing on the monkey bars all alone for 15 minutes. And there are the dreaded group projects for which no one asks your child to join a group.

For you, there is filling out the school emergency information form and not having anyone's name to put down as a contact person. (I remember arguing with a school secretary who told me I *had* to put a local person's name as an emergency contact. Finally I asked her what her name was, because—after talking with her for five minutes—I now knew her better than anyone else in the city. She decided I could leave the line blank.) There are the sports team practices in which all the other parents remember one another from last year. And there are those trips to the grocery store or to the pharmacy where you don't see one face that you recognize.

Remember these feelings once you are a part of the group. Know that other newcomers feel the same way, and don't assume somebody else will help them feel welcome. Take the initiative yourself to seek out and welcome newcomers. Help your children understand the importance of doing the same thing. And if long-time neighbors don't reach out to you, take the first step to get to know them, too.

The rest of the country could learn a lot about hospitality from places like Louisville and Atlanta. When we moved to those cities, our new neighbors greeted us warmly, generally with a plate of home-baked cookies. I have since adopted that practice to welcome newcomers everywhere that we have lived. And even though the idea occasionally seems foreign to some of the recipients of my hospitality, I haven't yet had anyone refuse the cookies! More important than the cookies is the note card I provide my new neighbors; it lists the names of my family members, my kids' ages, and our phone number. I encourage the newcomers to call me if they have questions about where to find stores, what doctors to use, how to enroll in sports programs, and so on. I also give them a personal invitation to neighborhood get-togethers and offer to accompany them to the first event.

> "Last year about a week before my birthday party, a new girl came into my American history class. I made a point of talking to her and inviting her to my party. We had a great time, and all of my friends enjoyed getting to meet someone new."
>
> REBECCA, AGE 14

After one of our moves, we had been in our new house for several weeks and still hadn't met some of the couples with grown children that lived on our street. I was excited one afternoon when the doorbell rang and I could see through the glass a delivery person with a large arrangement of flowers. To my disappointment, the delivery person told me the flowers weren't for me (I hate when that happens!), but rather were for my next-door neighbor, who would be getting home from the hospital soon. Although this was one of the neighbors that I hadn't met, I told the delivery person I'd be happy to deliver the flowers later that afternoon. Seeing an opportunity to be neighborly, I whipped up a batch of chocolate-chip cookies and delivered them along with the flowers.

There could be a myriad of reasons that established neighbors

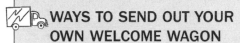

WAYS TO SEND OUT YOUR OWN WELCOME WAGON

Take cookies or other homemade treats to your new neighbors.

Give your new neighbors a note card with your name, your phone number, and the names and ages of your children.

Offer to be the emergency contact on the school information form for a child new to your neighborhood.

Invite children moving in to your neighborhood to play at your house while their parents unpack boxes.

Host a party to welcome a new child on your street.

Invite families new to the neighborhood to go with your family to neighborhood get-togethers or local events.

Introduce yourself and your children to long-time residents who don't reach out to you first.

Encourage your children to invite new students at school to birth-day parties and other get-togethers.

Prepare a packet for your new neighbors with business cards from dependable service providers (such as a pediatrician, a dentist, an electrician, and a plumber) and takeout menus from your favorite local restaurants. Add brochures from organizations that serve kids, such as the public library, the YMCA, and the Boys and Girls Club.

don't attempt to introduce themselves—illness, shyness, respect for privacy, previous bad experiences, or just a lack of awareness that new people have moved in. Don't assume they are unfriendly people who don't want to get to know you and your children. Rather, take the first step to initiate a relationship with them. If they choose not to be friendly after that, at least you'll know you've done your part.

Despite the fact that it sometimes makes them uncomfortable, my kids are generally pretty good about welcoming newcomers to the neighborhood. They often accompany me on my cookie deliveries to find out how old the new neighbors are. If there are children close to their ages, they invite them over to play right away. And we maintain a "What's one more?" philosophy when it comes to birthday party invitations. Even though I generally establish a maximum number of invitees, my children know we'll always make an exception if a new neighbor or student comes into the picture.

Nothing will help a child's transition more than immediately feeling that she has a group to which she belongs. Whether it's your child or the child of the school's or neighborhood's newest family, go out of your way to make sure he feels welcome. And if an established family in the neighborhood doesn't reach out to you when you move, send out your own welcome wagon. Hidden within the new kid at school or the neighbors who keep to themselves could be a meaningful new friendship for your children or for your whole family.

21

Don't forget to take care of yourself.

Go confidently in the direction of your dreams!
Live the life you've imagined.
—Henry David Thoreau

Occasionally, one of those irritating e-mail messages that travel around the world about every six months contains something witty enough to make me chuckle. One that always brings a grin is a rule "that little children have learned: When your mom is mad at your dad, don't let her brush your hair." Along those lines are the words of the famous flea-market kitchen plaque: "If Mama ain't happy, ain't nobody happy." These witticisms make me laugh because there is truth to them. The mood of the primary caregiver truly sets the tone for the rest of the family.

This is why it is essential that parents take care of themselves, particularly when facing the stress of a move. For too many parents—moms particularly—life seems to be a series of sacrifices for the children. For the most part, I think, this is because parents truly do want the best for their children and are willing to make sacrifices to see that they get it. There is nothing wrong with this. In fact, making sacrifices is admirable as long as parents don't lose their sense of identity and self-worth in the process. But what are you teaching your children if you don't care enough about yourself to eat right? Or exercise regularly? Or stay sober? Or develop your own social-support system? Or take some time each day to relax? Or follow your dreams? I know that a lot of parents feel guilty when they take time away from their children to take care of themselves; I struggle with this, too. But I also recognize that by taking care of ourselves we parents can better care for our children.

An added benefit of meeting one's own needs is that in so doing you may open doors for your children. My children have become friends with the children of many of the women in my monthly bunco group. In other women's groups, I've scoped out moms with children similar in age to my own. When I introduce myself, our children and their interests are ready-made topics of conversation. These conversations have frequently resulted in get-togethers and subsequent friendships between our children.

One of Laurie's favorite things to do to relax is scrapbooking. To meet both her needs and those of her children, she often hosts "Mommy and Me Scrapbooking Parties," in which children are invited to attend with their moms and to share in this fun activity. In one of her previous communities, Laurie participated in a women's Bible study group that met in members' homes; children were welcome to come along and to cultivate their own friendships while the moms studied together. Similarly, many communities have Newcomers' Clubs, which couple monthly meetings for adults with family-friendly activities. Groups like these are ideal for meeting both kids' and parents' social needs.

After her divorce, Connie had to decide how to balance her needs with those of her children. Shortly after she moved to Nashville, some strangers knocked on her door and handed her printed information about activities at a nearby church. She wasn't particularly interested, because she had already chosen a local church of her own denomination, until the visitors invited her to attend a weekly divorcees' support group that was starting the following week. Connie could think of many reasons not to attend:

She didn't know anyone, she would have to arrange babysitting for her boys, and the whole idea of attending such meetings made her uncomfortable. But Connie also felt that the group might provide something she needed during this difficult period of her life.

To Connie's pleasant surprise, not only did the divorcees' support group prove to be a valuable resource for her, but it also directly benefited her sons. She told the group that Christmas would be difficult for her family financially as well as emotionally. Touched by her situation, they rallied other members of the church to shower Connie's family with Christmas gifts and gift certificates. This out-pouring of love and concern for her family would not have happened had Connie not been willing to risk participating in this group. As she explains, "I had to be willing to be vulnerable, to let people know what our needs were, both emotionally and financially. It was so hard to speak out and let our needs be known—but it was so important for me to do that for myself and for my children."

> "It's hard to find the time, but I know that taking care of myself when I move is so important. Scrapbooking is my favorite form of relaxation, so sometimes I invite a friend and her daughter over to scrapbook. It's great, because we get mommy time and they get kid time together."
>
> LAURIE, MOTHER OF TWO

When my family moved to Fort Lauderdale, I decided to do something for myself that has had lasting benefits for my children. Weight was a demon with which I'd struggled my whole life. I had tried every fad diet, plus some healthy ones, but it seemed that for every 10 pounds I'd take off I'd eventually put 15 back on. *Obese* would be the appropriate word to describe me as we made our first move to Florida. So I decided that I would use this move not only to spend more time with the children but also as an opportunity to tackle my weight problem once and for all. I decided to forgo the enticing fad diets and change my lifestyle instead. After 11 months of exercising for at least 40 minutes six times a week and following the Weight Watchers healthy eating plan, I reached my goal weight, losing 74 pounds. And I am pleased to report that—nine years later—I have maintained that loss.

By taking care of myself and getting my weight down to a healthy level, I gave my children several priceless gifts. I gave them a mom who has the energy to keep up with them and their countless activities. I taught them that I care enough about myself to take care of the body God gave me. And I've taught them how to maintain a healthy lifestyle. Now every member of our family is expected to get regular exercise. Although we don't deny our passion for anything chocolate, we eat sweets in moderation and fruits and vegetables every day. We're so used to eating low-fat versions of traditional dishes that my kids actually prefer my fat-free mashed potatoes (made with skim milk and fat-free sour cream) to the buttery mashed potatoes that other families make. And we all spend some time each day reading, writing in a journal, or relaxing in some other way.

What do you need to do to take care of yourself? Do you need social support to help you feel less disconnected after a move? Do you need to treat your body better by losing weight or exercising regularly? Do you need the spiritual support of a small group at your church, temple, or mosque? If your brain feels like mush from being around preschoolers all day, do you need the intellectual stimulation of a book club or seminar? Have you always dreamed of writing a novel, and do you need to set aside some time every day to bring this dream to fruition?

Caring for your children shouldn't mean giving up your own goals and dreams. You will be better able to care for your children if you replenish yourself emotionally, physically, socially, and spiritually. Use the move as a chance to commit to taking care of yourself. You'll be doing a favor for your children as well as for yourself.

22

Keep in touch with old friends.

A friend is the hope of the heart.
—Ralph Waldo Emerson

Of all the tips in this book, this may be the most important one in helping your children deal with the grief that accompanies a move. Children need to understand that, when they have developed a special friendship with someone, it doesn't have to end because they move away. The form of the friendship will change drastically—there will be no more of those unplanned, everyday activities that help build a bond between two people. But there is no reason that genuine friendships can't last a lifetime.

Today's technology makes maintaining contact with friends across the country much easier than in the past. Rebecca has friends in Baltimore and Topeka with whom she converses through an instant-messaging program almost every day. They can exchange pictures within seconds, and they have introduced one another to other friends online (of course, family rules about Internet use are critical to ensure safety). I keep in contact with friends from my various adult and childhood homes through the

Internet; these friends include Debby, from Baltimore, who moved to Germany at the same time we moved to Tampa. The Internet is a wonderful tool for inexpensively maintaining regular contact with faraway friends.

But the type of contact I'm referring to in this chapter goes beyond haphazard Internet communication. Keeping important friendships vital after you have moved requires deliberate effort. For young children, this means deliberate effort on the part of the parents as well as the kids. Have them send letters and holiday cards to each other and exchange photos; e-mail can't beat the excitement of opening the mailbox and finding a letter from a best friend. If your kids are reluctant to write, let them pick out stationery for either handwritten notes or the computer. Children who are too young to write can just draw a picture and dictate a short message. Besides encouraging letter writing, let your children call their friends periodically to talk about important things going on in their lives. Hearing each other's voices and keeping apprised of major events in each other's lives are critical to keeping a long-distance relationship intimate. For special friends, maintaining contact may go beyond letters and phone calls; sending birthday and holiday presents is a fun way to help your children show their friends that they are thinking about them.

> "My best friend in the world, Alex, lives in Kansas. Every summer she comes to my house to visit. In one week, we are able to catch up on a year's worth of events. . . . I always wish that she would never have to leave."
>
> SARAH, AGE 13

Sometimes kids themselves come up with creative ways to keep a friendship dynamic after a move. When we lived in Baltimore, the kids on our street formed a group called the Badogs. They actually started out as a street hockey team, but when the only team they could find to play against consisted of older boys who beat them by 17 goals, they decided to become a soft-rock band instead. They spent hours making up and singing songs, and even performed at the block party before we left. Sarah and her Badog friend Brittani decided to keep the Badogs alive after we moved to Tampa by writing an adventure series, "Badogs Forever," based loosely on their exploits. Sarah would write a few paragraphs of the story and then e-mail it to Brittani, who would add a few paragraphs, e-mail it back to Sarah, and so forth.

The best way to maintain a friendship, if at all possible, is to visit each other. Let me add a cautionary note: You must not promise your children that they can visit their friends after a move if you're not going to follow through. If you know your children won't be able to go back and visit, be honest with them about this. Their disappointment will not be as great as the resentment they would feel later if you failed to keep your word. Mary, a military mom, says that her kids don't let her get away with empty promises: "My kids are good. They nail me down. . . . They want specifics on *when* they can visit their friends."

My family tries to visit most of the places we've lived within one or two years of moving away. This helps our transition in two ways. First, we get to see our old friends, catch up on their lives, and demonstrate to them that we still consider them an important part of our lives. Second, visiting helps us see that life in the old community has indeed moved on without us. With each trip we've made, as much as we've enjoyed spending time with our old friends, we have confirmed for ourselves that our former community is no longer our home. The contrast between our former community and our new one helps us realize that we, too, have moved on; we now have a new home.

While living in Topeka, Rebecca and Sarah each found a soul mate. You know, the kind of friend with whom there is an immediate connection, who can finish your sentences for you, and who knows immediately when you're upset, no matter how hard you try to hide it. Sarah was only in first grade when she became friends with Alex, and Becca was in third grade when she and Lindsey became friends. Seven years later, both pairs of girls are still close friends. Because these friendships were so intense before we left Topeka, Alex's and Lindsey's mothers and I committed to doing

> "Because military families move so frequently, my friends and I have learned to exchange our parents' phone numbers and addresses. This has helped me find family friends after a forwarding address has expired."
>
> LAURIE, MOTHER OF TWO

what we could to let the girls see each other at least once a year.

Since then, Alex and Lindsey's week-long summer visits have become one of our family's most anticipated events. The first summer, we drove 1,100 miles from Baltimore to Topeka for a visit, and then brought Alex and Lindsey home with us. Before we started for home, Randy and I weren't sure that driving 19 hours with five kids in our minivan would be the smartest thing to do, but the girls' excitement and anticipation made the trip seem easy and quick. Lindsey had never seen mountains before, so we stopped for photos several times along the way. Once we got home, we did a few special activities, including a day-long sightseeing tour of Washington, D.C., but most of the time the four girls just played at

 FUN WAYS TO KEEP IN TOUCH WITH OLD FRIENDS

Write letters regularly.

Schedule regular times for instant-messaging.

Exchange school and family photos.

Exchange birthday and holiday cards or presents.

Start a traveling journal. Take turns writing in it, and mail it back and forth.

Telephone each other regularly.

Compose stories together through e-mail.

Go back with your family to your former community for a long visit.

Plan a shared vacation for two families.

Invite a best friend for a week-long summer visit, and host a party during the visit so the old friend can meet some new friends.

our house, doing the things they did every day when they lived in the same town. At the end of the week, we took Lindsey and Alex to the airport for their flight home. As they said their goodbyes, the girls agreed that, although they miss being together every day, getting to spend an entire week together, exploring a new part of the country, wouldn't have happened if we still lived in Topeka.

> **"I keep my people *hot* [in my heart]."**
>
> SAM, AGE 3

To help the girls remember their adventures, I put together a scrapbook for each girl (including Becca and Sarah) filled with photographs and other mementos of their activities. At the end of each scrapbook, I wrote a note telling them how glad I was that they were best friends. "I know you really miss each other," I wrote, "but always remember: Even 1,100 miles can't separate true friends."

These visits are highlights of the year for all four of the girls, and rarely have they missed one in seven years. In many ways, the girls' friendships have become closer and even more special because of the opportunities afforded them when we moved away.

If you move often, maintaining contact with friends from each location becomes a challenge. We have had to prioritize our trips, knowing that we can't visit all five of the places we have lived as often as we would like. If your situation is similar, give your friends a standing invitation to visit you. Many of our old friends have visited our home in Florida, and we spent the children's spring break last year in Miami with two families who had been our neighbors in Baltimore (one of them has since moved to New Jersey and the other to South Carolina). Our commitment to staying connected with friends around the country has been critical to our satisfaction with each move. By helping your children maintain connections with the friends they have to leave behind, you will help them weave an important part of their past into their new lives.

23

Model a positive attitude.

> *Wherever you find yourself is*
> *exactly where you need to be.*
> —Iyanla Vanzant

In dealing with an onslaught of gripes and conflicts among employees, a former boss and I concluded that we could classify most people into one of two categories: energy drainers and energy generators. Energy drainers spend too much time complaining about things without offering resolutions, take no responsibility for their mistakes, and view situations in the worst possible light. Energy generators, in contrast, offer creative solutions to problems, fully own up to the consequences of their actions, and keep problems in perspective.

Modeling a positive attitude for your children—or, in other words, being an energy generator—is critical during a move, and especially afterward, when it is normal for a family to go through an adjustment period in which both the children and adults feel dissatisfaction with some aspect of the experience. Energy drainers have more difficulty than others in moving beyond this adjustment period. In my experience, children and teenagers who are very dissatisfied with a move a year or more later have at least one parent who approached the move with resignation. I'm sure you've heard adults make such comments as these: "I knew we'd never like this place." "We're never going to be happy here." "We'll never be able to make friends like the ones we had in our last neighborhood." "This will never feel like home." These people are so convinced they won't like their new community that they are not even willing to give it a try. Their prophecies of misery become self-fulfilling. Not only does their attitude make life harder on them, it also makes an already stressful situation even harder on their children.

Energy-generating parents help their children cope with a move by expecting a positive experience, by taking full responsibility for their part in the decision to move, and by maintaining a sense of humor. My childhood friend Sherry Tinsley Martinez is one of the most positive people I know. She feels blessed that God has given her two special sons, 16-year-old Cooper, who has Down syndrome, and 12-year-old Clay, who has been diagnosed with Asperger's syndrome. Sherry and her family recently moved out of Indiana for the first time in her adult life to settle in Nebraska—900 miles away—to be closer to her new step-granddaughter. Because of Sherry's energy-generating personality, I had no doubt that she and her family would quickly adjust to their new home. Sure enough, within a few weeks of the move Sherry excitedly informed me that Cooper was already involved in Special Olympics, Clay was doing well in school, they had found a church, and they were enjoying the local high-school football games and rodeos.

Although I haven't started out each move as enthusiastic as Sherry, I now know in my heart that my family could move anywhere and eventually everything would work out okay for us. I know that the kids would make new friends, do well in school, and get to know our neighbors, and that we soon would feel that the new community was our home. These things have happened with every move. No matter how apprehensive you feel about moving, you'll help your children by maintaining the conviction that you will make the best of your family's new situation.

I personally take this philosophy a step further: Like Iyanla Vanzant, I believe that we are exactly where we need to be at any moment in time. There is a reason that circumstances have led us to each place where we have lived. Each person we have met, each experience we have had, has changed our lives in ways that could not have happened if we hadn't been willing to move. A good example of this occurred when my family moved to Tampa.

> "Moving isn't always as scary as it seems."
>
> REBECCA, AGE 14

To say that I didn't want to leave Baltimore would be putting it mildly. We had stayed in each of our three prior homes only 16 months, so during our three years in Baltimore we had planted what felt like very deep roots. The kids were happy, we had many great friends, we had built our dream house, and Randy was finally at a point in his career where he could turn down promotions and still have job security. We were totally unprepared when, in the aftermath of the terrorist attacks on September 11, 2001, a corporate restructuring forced us to move so that Randy could keep his job.

One benefit of moving to the Tampa area was that we were now about an hour's drive north of my grandparents, whose closest relatives until then had been more than 800 miles away. Five months after we moved, my grandmother had a debilitating stroke. She was moved to a nursing home, and she passed away seven months later. Through frequent visits during those seven months, my children and I were able to get to know my grandparents more intimately than had been possible during our annual visits in the past. The kids brought homemade cards or cookies, and Becca occasionally played her flute for her great-grandmother. As I drove home in silence from the hospital the night my grandmother died, I pondered how fortunate my children and I were to have been able to spend so much time with her during her last few months. It dawned on me that our move to Tampa had brought us to exactly the place we needed to be, at the right time. Had we stayed in Baltimore, we would have missed this last opportunity for my children to get to know their wonderful great-grandmother.

As I was preparing to write this book, I realized I hadn't done a very good job in practicing the second energy-generating habit: taking full responsibility for my role in the decision to move. Every time we had uprooted our family and said goodbye to cherished friends, a part of me had been angry about it. What was Randy's company thinking in asking us to make three moves in a row after we'd lived in each of our homes for only 16 months? Didn't Randy's bosses care that we had three children who were attached to their friends and schools? It was easier to point the finger of blame at Randy's company than to own up to the fact that each move was actually our choice. We may have seen the consequences of not moving as undesirable (Randy wouldn't be able to advance any further in his career) or even unaccept-able (Randy could lose his job), but moving was still our choice. And just as it is our responsibility, as parents, to make the choice about each move according to the best inter-ests of our family, it is the responsibility of Randy's employer, as a business accountable to its stockholders, to make choices about who should be promoted and when accord-ing to the best interests of the company. The acknowledgment that we weren't victims forced me to take responsibility for each move and the effects it has had on our fami-ly's life.

Giving up feeling like a victim was an important step for me. Although I had never let my resentment stop me from turning each move into a positive experience, I could have done this sooner if I had had the self-awareness that I now have. I don't want my children to believe that Randy and I are vic-tims in situations in which we really do have control. Believing that, they might tend to see themselves as victims, too. An impor-tant part of children's development is understanding that they

> "I tell my sons that attitude is a choice. We can choose to consider the move as a new adventure and look forward to what can be, or we can choose to be sad and regret what we are missing. We need to choose to be involved, to make ourselves vulnerable, to go out on a limb and try new things. It's important to look at what changes this move will enable in our lives, not what changes it is forcing upon us."
>
> CONNIE, SINGLE
> MOTHER OF FOUR BOYS

have more choices in life than they may think, that they are responsible for their choices, and that every choice has consequences.

If anyone has ever had the right to feel like a victim, Connie did. Not only did she have to accept that what she thought was a happy marriage had abruptly ended, but she also was suddenly forced to assume financial responsibility for her four sons and herself. Connie could have easily dug a hole of self-pity and buried herself and her sons in it. Instead, she chose to make the best of the situation and to encourage her sons to look upon their subsequent move as a new adventure. During family meetings following the move, Connie emphasized to her sons that they would adjust most easily by focusing on changes the move would enable them to make in their lives, not on changes the move was forcing upon them.

Finally, I can't overemphasize the importance of keeping your sense of humor during a move. A good example is our family's reaction to the Sleeping Beauty pajamas fiasco described in chapter 20. We saw nothing funny about the incident as it was happening;

 WAYS TO MODEL A POSITIVE ATTITUDE FOR YOUR CHILDREN

Expect the move to be a good experience.

Avoid pointing out ways that your new home fails to measure up to your old one.

Look for the new opportunities that this move will bring about in your lives.

Take full responsibility for your part in the decision to move.

Find things to laugh about.

Cultivate a sense of adventure and belonging in your new home.

Sarah felt humiliated, and Randy and I were embarrassed. We were angry that the other moms and the dance instructors didn't do something to rectify the situation before the curtain went up. The next day, however, Randy and I just looked at each other a few times, shook our heads, and chuckled, wondering how we could have had such rotten luck. By the following week, the whole family was laughing together at the memory of that dreadful moment when the curtain first rose. As we recount the story now to friends, we all laugh hysterically and wonder how we could have survived such an embarrassing event.

Life is full of embarrassing moments. You can choose either to let them paralyze you or to see the humor in them and move on. Of course, it is critical not to use humor to minimize your children's feelings or to try to get them to stop feeling sad when the hurt is fresh. For example, telling Sarah to get over her embarrassment and see the humor in the pajamas incident immediately after it happened would have been inappropriate. Or, when children are dealing with the pain of a move, trying to get them to laugh while they are expressing their feelings will give them the message that it's not okay to feel sad. In the right time and place, though, humor is a great tool for helping us deal with life's stresses.

Laughter may truly be the best medicine. It has been proven that laughing (as well as chocolate and exercise) releases endorphins, brain chemicals that make us feel good and reduce pain. Studies have shown that laughter can help release tension, improve breathing, lower blood pressure, build relationships, relieve depression, improve brain functioning, and possibly even help prevent heart disease.

When your children are feeling down before or after a move, find something to laugh about. Rent a funny video. Pull out the baby pictures. Take turns doing impressions of your favorite lines from movies or songs. When our family needs a good laugh, we often pull out the journal I keep of the cute things the kids have said (remember, the one my friend recommended I start?). Here are some entries related to moves that make us laugh:

With four-year-old Mark in the car, I followed the girls' bus on the first day of school in Topeka, and then we waited in the hallway while they got off the bus. When Mark noticed the principal pacing the halls and peering into each classroom, Mark tugged on my sleeve and whispered, "I think that's the president."

Sarah, at seven, singing at the top of her lungs in our new Topeka home: "Home, home on the range. Where the deer and the cantaloupe play."

The first time we took the kids to the site where our Baltimore house was being built, the girls admired the yard and the foundation that had just been poured. Mark, age five, was unimpressed until his gaze fell upon a small structure in the front yard. Tugging my arm excitedly, Mark exclaimed with wide eyes, "Look, Mom, we have a port-a-potty at our new house!"

Although these stories probably don't make you double over with hilarity, they amuse our family. I'm sure you have amusing family stories, too. By learning to see the humor in everyday situations, each of my children has developed a wonderful sense of humor that keeps Randy and me continually amused. From the time they were born, I would make jokes that went way over the kids' heads—just to amuse myself. Now that they get most of my jokes (even if they insist that most of them aren't funny), life has become even more amusing. Give your children the precious gift of humor. It will help them cope during the stress of a move and throughout their lives.

24

Use storytelling to celebrate your family history.

*Every moment that's ever been, or ever will be,
is gone the instant it's begun. So life is loss. And
the secret of happiness is to learn to love the
moment more than you mourn the loss.*

—Dan Baker, *What Happy People Know*

When I was seven months pregnant with Sarah, and Rebecca was 18 months old, we started a family storytelling ritual that we continued for almost a decade. Once *Goodnight Moon*, *Love You Forever*, and the other favorite books of the moment were read and prayers were said, I would tell the story of the Burgan family. It went like this:

Once upon a time there were a mommy and a daddy, and they loved each other very much. So Mommy and Daddy decided to get married, and they became a family. They were a family for many years—just Mommy and Daddy—and they were very happy. Then one day they decided that they loved each other so much that they wanted to share their love with a baby. So Mommy and Daddy made a baby, and the baby was in Mommy's belly. And the baby grew and grew, and Mommy's belly got bigger and bigger. Finally it was time for the baby to come out of Mommy's belly. So Mommy and Daddy went to the hospi-

tal, and the doctor helped take the baby out of Mommy's belly. And it was a beautiful *baby girl, the most beautiful baby girl Mommy and Daddy had ever seen. And they named that baby girl . . .* (at this point Becca would remove her pacifier and, with shining eyes and a heart-warming smile, finish the sentence: *Becca!*). *Yes, they named that baby girl Rebecca Marie Burgan. And they were a family— just Mommy, Daddy, and Becca—and they were very happy. And then one day they decided they loved one another so much that they wanted to share that love with another baby, so they made another baby, and that baby is in Mommy's belly right now.*

Our family story grew, as we added Sarah Catherine and later Mark Collins to the family and then began our moving history. But no matter who was in our family or where our family lived, the con-

> "My kids are proud that they have lived so many places and have had such diverse experiences. It's an important part of who they are and who we are as a family."
>
> MARY, MOTHER OF FOUR

stants were the love and the joy that we brought to one another. What started out as an improvised story to help Becca fall asleep one evening stood the test of time because it not only helped our children feel loved, but it also gave them a sense of belonging, a sense of family identity. Even before my kids could comprehend the meaning of this story with their minds, they understood it with their hearts.

I talked in chapter 17 about the importance of creating a sense of belonging in your new community. Even more fundamental for children is to cultivate their sense of belonging in their family. It is important for children to understand the richness of their family history—to appreciate the strengths and contributions of their parents, grandparents, and those who came before them. When Becca and I get the giggles at an inappropriate moment, I tell her stories of how Great-Grandmother Collins would sometimes do the same thing—in church, when Great-Grandfather Collins was preaching! When Sarah says something witty, I remind her of witticisms Great-Grandmother Jeune would make to keep us all laughing. Reminding children of their heritage and of how their ancestors are kept alive through them helps develop their sense of self-worth and of belonging to a family unit larger than themselves.

Likewise, it is important for children to know their immediate family's history. For families who have moved, this means periodically talking about why the family moved, what the old home and community were like, who the children's friends were, and what activities the children enjoyed. Having these talks is particularly important if visits to your former community are impractical.

Spending time looking at old photographs together is an easy way to begin a family discussion on your moving history. Photos often spark "remember when" stories that can go on for hours. Remember when Sarah dressed up like Abraham Lincoln for her report on presidents at Westminster Elementary? Remember when Mark and Brett made perfect three-year-old friends, because Mark couldn't pronounce his *s*'s and Brett said enough *s*'s for both of them? Remember when Becca had all the girls from her third-grade class over for a slumber party and they danced and giggled all night?

Home videos offer another wonderful opportunity to celebrate your family's past. At the beginning of every summer, one of my kids starts pulling out the family videos. One by one, we all stop

---

WAYS TO CELEBRATE YOUR FAMILY HISTORY

Spend time together looking at old photos.

Pop some popcorn, and watch home videos.

Create photojournals (picture albums with descriptive notes).

Talk about the places you've lived and your old friends.

Create digital family stories, combining written and oral narrative with images and music.

what we're doing, and we end up having a video marathon. How we love to remember what the kids looked like, how they talked, what clothes they wore, what mannerisms they had—and to notice which characteristics have stayed the same. And how meaningful it is to watch the children interact with their friends in each place we've lived, remember what our homes looked like, and relive all our happy memories.

Some parents of families who have moved a lot don't like their kids to watch home videos or look at old photos because, the parents feel, these pictures unearth painful memories. My children and I often feel a twinge of sadness at remembering what we've left behind. But the joy we feel at how fortunate we were to have all those experiences far exceeds the sadness. As Dan Baker wrote, "The secret of happiness is to learn to love the moment more than you mourn the loss." We must not be so afraid of letting our children feel sadness that we ignore opportunities to help them savor some wonderful memories.

> "I really get upset about leaving my house and my friends behind when we move. What helps is looking at the pictures of my friends in the scrapbook that my mom makes."
>
> MATTHEW, AGE 10

Laurie, a military mom, helps her children remember their family history through photojournaling. Laurie showed me the photojournal she had created during their three years in Germany; more than 120 pages long, it represents everything her family did during three years of their lives. Every holiday, every first day of school, every friend, every vacation, even seemingly insignificant daily events while living in Germany are chronicled by photographs in the album. Next to each picture, Laurie has written notes about its subject. Laurie has found this photojournal to be a great source of comfort to her children when they are missing their friends.

Digital storytelling is a new way of making family storytelling fun. Online resources are available to help you celebrate your family history through a combination of narrative, images, music, and voice. A quick Internet search for "digital storytelling" will provide numerous resources you can explore with your children to celebrate your family's past in a technologically savvy way.

Through stories, photographs, home videos, journaling, digital storytelling, or any other methods that are meaningful for your family, you help your children understand what an important role moving has played in their family history. Celebrate how the places they have lived and the people they have met have helped shape their individual personalities and your family's lifestyle, values, and traditions.

25

View the experience as a new beginning.

*Each day the world is born anew
for him who takes it rightly.*
—James Russell Lowell

A long with the excitement that surrounds the Super Bowl each
year comes the anticipation about which commercials will
end up being classics. My favorite in 2005 involved a series of
well-known people associated with the NFL (such as Dallas Cow-
boys owner Jerry Jones, Pittsburgh Steelers quarterback Ben
Roethlisberger, Oakland Raiders defensive tackle Warren Sapp,
and Tampa Bay Buccaneers coach John Gruden) singing, off-key,
"Tomorrow," from the musical *Annie*. It is notable as you are watching that neither of the teams playing in the Super Bowl is repre-
sented in the commercial. The tagline was "As of tomorrow, we're
all undefeated again."

In this sense, a move is like the Super Bowl. When you move, you
give yourself a fresh start, a new beginning. The start of life in your
new home is kind of like the beginning of my weekly tennis set,
when my friend Vicki and I are equals. Then she beats me, and we
start a new set—again as equals. A move gives you an opportunity
to forget about your previous score and start over.

Maybe your children have been considering making some personal changes—in the way they spend their time or the way they look, for instance. A move may be a good time to try something new. Perhaps your daughter has been doing gymnastics for years and would like to try dance classes instead (just watch out for those recitals!). Maybe your son plays the guitar and is now interested in learning percussion. My daughter Sarah, who spends most of her free time playing sports, has long blond hair that she ties back in a ponytail. When we first moved to Tampa, she seriously contemplated getting a very short haircut. She reasoned that no one she saw outside of the family would know that she had ever worn her hair another way, so she wouldn't have to deal with stares and snide remarks. Although at the last minute she decided against cutting her hair, this would have been a good time to make the change.

Just after a move may be a good time for a child to try out a new sport, perhaps one that is popular in your new community but not in your old one. If it's your first time in a cold climate, encourage your children to learn to ice-skate or ski. If you move to a community near the beach, try surfing or sailing. If your children lack confidence as athletes, get them some special training in the sport of choice before signing them up for a team.

Maybe your child would like to change a personality trait, such as shyness. Many children overcome shyness as they make new friends after a move, and success in making friends often gives them the confidence to be more assertive in other areas of their lives. As Mary told herself when she moved as a child, no one in her new community knew she was shy, so moving was a great opportunity to pretend that she was outgoing. Some children need to work on being more considerate, or more honest, or more responsible. Tell your children that moving is an opportunity to reinvent themselves as considerate or honest or responsible people. Provide specific guidance, for example, by teaching them manners or reminding them to do their homework.

If your children are older, maybe they need to make some lifestyle changes. If they became couch potatoes in their former residence, can they commit to exercising regularly at your new home? If your teenager often insisted on sleeping in instead of going to religious services before you moved, can you resume attending services as a family? Encourage your children to view the move as a chance to change their ways for the better.

Some children may need to make drastic changes in their lives. Maybe your daughter has gotten involved with the wrong crowd, with kids who drink or take drugs. She can enter a new school with no one knowing about her past. Maybe your son is the favorite target of the neighborhood bully. The kids in your new community won't necessarily view him as someone to pick on. Maybe your daughter was expelled from school for getting in a fight. Her reputation as a troublemaker does not need to follow her to her new community.

> "My dad was in the Army, so our family moved a lot when I was a child. My sisters always felt I handled moving better than the rest of them. I just looked upon moving as an opportunity to try new skills with new people. I was basically shy by nature, but I would remind myself that no one in the place I was moving to knew I was shy."
>
> MARY, MOTHER OF FOUR

When your child makes a commitment to do better, it is important that you support him in his efforts. For example, if your son is slow in school or picked on because of his immaturity, you might have him repeat a year, which he could do in a new town without anyone knowing, or you could get him some tutoring before he starts at the new school. If your daughter hasn't been taking school seriously because the classes lack challenge or inspiration, make sure the new school is a better one, or have her skip a year (again, without other children knowing). If your child has been getting into trouble out of boredom, maybe you and he together could get involved in a new activity, such as scouting, 4-H, or search-and-rescue.

If major behavioral changes are needed, you may want to have your child work with a professional counselor before or after the move. Unless the root causes of the problems are addressed, your children will likely find themselves falling into similar patterns in their new community. But if you use the move as an opportunity to couple professional guidance with a commitment to improving behavior, a move can serve as the perfect vehicle for giving your child a fresh start.

While you are encouraging your children to make positive changes in their lives, don't forget to do the same for yourself. What aspects of your life would you like to change? In some ways, a move lets you start life over. As I described in chapter 21, the biggest change I've made after a move was beginning to exercise and to eat healthily; this resulted in a dramatic weight loss and subsequent maintenance of that loss. Losing weight has truly given me a fresh start. Friends I've made since this change are surprised when I tell them the story. When they look at me they don't see the "baggage" (pardon the pun) that I used to carry. I took advantage of a move to clean my slate and reinvent myself. I still carry my "before" picture in my purse as a reminder that I have accepted responsibility for my health and appearance.

A move always brings some pain and sadness. Through a move, though, you and your children can experience life-changing benefits that otherwise might not have been possible. Embrace your move. Take every opportunity to turn your fresh beginning into a happy ending.

Index